"Buyers are fried, frazzled, and frenetic. Jill Konrath took that 'obvious' insight and rewrote the book on selling. Turns out it has massive ramifications for consultative selling, how you communicate, and your entire sales process. *SNAP Selling* is more than a good acronym—it's a sales book for our times."
—Charles H. Green, CEO,
Trusted Advisor Associates, and author of *Trust-based Selling*

"Wake up! In today's economy, your sales team is your primary competitive advantage—not your products or services. *SNAP Selling* clearly articulates the knowledge and skills they need to dominate the market." —Mary Delaney, CEO, Personified

"This book artfully reveals the key insights every salesperson or sales exec better know if they want to be a top producer today."
—Chet Holmes, author of *The Ultimate Sales Machine*

"*SNAP Selling* is a Sales 2.0 survival guide for this decade. In it, Jill blends her years of selling experience, sharp wit, and Midwestern sensibility to create a valuable resource for the modern sales professional."
—Rand Schulman, chief marketing officer, InsideView

"Jill Konrath has written the definitive book on how to sell in an Internet-driven, time-pressured, information-overloaded world. Her truly innovative *SNAP Selling* strategies leave other sales models in the dust and are guaranteed to have your sales smokin' faster than you can say 'ready, aim, fire!'"
—Anne Miller, author of *Metaphorically Selling*

"Jill Konrath has done it again! *SNAP Selling* offers a clear strategy for how to reach, engage, and sell to today's hyper-connected, on-the-move business leaders. Kudos for showing us the road map."
—Razi Imam, founder, Landslide Technologies and 113 Industries

"Having a unique perspective on the sales performance and sales training business, I see Jill Konrath at the top of the heap when it comes to practical ideas, loyal followers, understanding of the critical selling issues today, and most important, relevance. I not only recommend her books, I recommend her."
—Dave Stein, CEO and founder, ES Research Group, Inc.

"Jill Konrath has an incredible gift that she shares in this book. By leveraging her vast sales wisdom, she delivers precise, relevant, and timely solutions that solve the most pressing challenges among today's sales force. Jill lasers in with pinpoint accuracy on the unique needs of today's sales professionals, providing them with selling strategies that shift personal productivity into hyper-drive, accelerate customer interest, and win more sales."

—Keith Rosen, executive sales coach and author of the award-winning *Coaching Salespeople into Sales Champions*

"As a corporate leader, time is my most precious commodity. If I'm working with a seller who has been smart enough to take the SNAP approach, I'm certain he or she will be better able to understand my priorities, communicate effectively, and respect my busy schedule. Read *SNAP Selling* and learn what it takes to become a priceless asset to your customers."

—Suzanne Sheppard, CEO, Executive Conversation, Inc.

"*SNAP Selling* is a mission-critical tool for building lasting, profitable relationships. Jill goes far beyond defining a sales process by rolling up her sleeves to share specifics about what you absolutely must do to become indispensable to your customer."

—Rick Pulito, vice president of sales, BI Worldwide

"Selling has changed radically and Jill Konrath has captured the essence of how to be successful in this new too-busy world. She's a master storyteller and a gifted seller. This book is filled with examples that'll make you stop your old-style selling and shift your approach to one of SNAP selling."

—Kendra Lee, president, KLA Group, and author of *More Hot Prospects*

"Sales organizations of tomorrow will need to be fundamentally different from those of today. *SNAP Selling* not only will radically change your thinking, it's one of those rare books that give you *actionable* strategies, steps, and examples that differentiate your approach and ultimately the value of your offering. For the next-generation sales force, this is a must-read!"

—Geoffrey Eitland, vice president of sales, Staples, Inc.

"At a time when executives face increased pressure to get more done in less time, Jill Konrath shows salespeople how to capture and keep the attention of these key decision makers. *SNAP Selling* is a real-world book from a real-world expert."

—Jim Fowler, CEO, Jigsaw

"For all the marketing and salespeople who haven't figured out how to adjust to buyers taking control, Jill Konrath clears that up in *SNAP Selling*. She doesn't just give you a high-level view, but rolls up her sleeves and provides practical approaches to put her on-target strategies into action."

—Ardath Albee, author of
eMarketing Strategies for the Complex Sale

"Jill Konrath gets what buyers deal with on a day-to-day basis and what keeps them from buying. In *SNAP Selling*, she shows salespeople how to cut through all the clutter and speed up the sales cycle. It's a must-read for new and veteran sellers."

—Ramon A. Avila, director, H.H. Gregg Center for Professional
Selling, Ball State University

"*SNAP Selling* is a game changer. Jill Konrath blasts traditional sales techniques and at the same time offers fresh insights and rock-solid advice that actually works in today's Sales 2.0 environment. It's provocative and practical."

—Jeanne Chapman, SVP and general manager, Corporate
Marketing Solutions, Entertainment Publications

"The art of selling has undergone more changes in the past few years than in any other time in history. *SNAP Selling* shows you how to capitalize on each one of them. Every new and experienced sales professional will find great value in this book. I strongly recommend it."

—Joseph Sugarman, chairman, BluBlocker Corporation

"SNAP is Straightforward, No-nonsense, Attuned, and Practical. Jill accurately reflects the realities of many buyers and offers helpful means of cutting through the noise and making the buyer/seller relationship work better for both parties."

—Mahan Khalsa, author of *Let's Get Real or Let's Not Play:
Transforming the Buyer/Seller Relationship*

"In *SNAP Selling*, Jill Konrath shows you a clear process that will help you to be highly relevant to your prospects and stand out from competitors. You'll discover numerous strategies for working smarter, engaging customers, and gaining more business."
—Lynn Schleeter, director, Center for Sales Innovation, St. Catherine University

"With the wealth of information available via the Internet, why does a prospect need a salesperson? Jill Konrath effectively deals with that question in *SNAP Selling*. While intuitively we may know that as the buy cycle changes, so too must the sell cycle, Jill lays out how to do that. Her blending of new insights and real-world examples makes *SNAP Selling* a must-read for all sales professionals." —Jim Dickie, managing partner, CSO Insights

"Jill addresses the realities of selling today and the sea change that has taken place. Not only does *SNAP Selling* clearly articulate what buyers expect from sellers, it also lays out a step-by-step plan on how to be relevant, add value, and move the sales process forward. Other sales books you read and put on the shelf, but this one you'll keep on your desk as a touchstone for effective selling." —Trish Bertuzzi, president, The Bridge Group, Inc.

SNAP SELLING

SNAP
SELLING

Speed Up Sales and
Win More Business with
Today's Frazzled Customers

JILL KONRATH

PORTFOLIO

PORTFOLIO

Published by the Penguin Group

Penguin Group (USA) Inc., 375 Hudson Street, New York, New York 10014, U.S.A.
Penguin Group (Canada), 90 Eglinton Avenue East, Suite 700, Toronto, Ontario, Canada
M4P 2Y3 (a division of Pearson Penguin Canada Inc.); Penguin Books Ltd, 80 Strand,
London WC2R 0RL, England; Penguin Ireland, 25 St. Stephen's Green, Dublin 2, Ireland
(a division of Penguin Books Ltd); Penguin Books Australia Ltd, 250 Camberwell Road,
Camberwell, Victoria 3124, Australia (a division of Pearson Australia Group Pty Ltd);
Penguin Books India Pvt Ltd, 11 Community Centre, Panchsheel Park, New Delhi—
110 017, India; Penguin Group (NZ), 67 Apollo Drive, Rosedale, North Shore 0632,
New Zealand (a division of Pearson New Zealand Ltd); Penguin Books (South Africa)
(Pty) Ltd, 24 Sturdee Avenue, Rosebank, Johannesburg 2196, South Africa

Penguin Books Ltd, Registered Offices:
80 Strand, London WC2R 0RL, England

First published in 2010 by Portfolio,
a member of Penguin Group (USA) Inc.

10 9 8 7 6 5 4 3 2 1

LIBRARY OF CONGRESS CATALOGING IN PUBLICATION DATA
Konrath, Jill.
   Snap selling : speed up sales and win more business with
today's frazzled customers / Jill Konrath.
       p.   cm.
   Includes index.
   ISBN 978-1-59184-330-6
   1. Selling. I. Title.
   HF5438.25.K662 2010
   658.85—dc22   2009053313

Printed in the United States of America
Set in Miller Text
Designed by Lucy Albanese

To my parents, Pat and Jack Ulseth,
for a lifetime of love,
a home filled with laughter,
and an unshakeable belief
in what's possible

CONTENTS

PART 2: The First Decision

PART 3: The Second Decision

PART 4: The Third Decision

PART 5: Wrapping It Up

SNAP SELLING

INTRODUCTION

You know what it's like to be crazy-busy. Before you're even fully awake in the morning, you're on the computer checking what seems like an endless stream of e-mail. When you look at your to-do list, you wonder how you'll be able to get everything done. You have a dozen people to follow up with on the phone, three meetings with prospects, and a proposal that needs to be finished. Then there's that nagging service issue that you can't seem to get resolved with that customer who's driving you nuts.

Rather than take a break for lunch, you grab a quick sandwich at the vending machine and eat it at your desk. That way you can update your files and take care of paperwork that needs to be processed. Then you head out for that presentation that you wish you'd had more time to prepare for. After the presentation, you have a ton of questions that now need to get answered before the end of the week. At least, that's what you promised your newest prospects.

By the time you get home, you're tired. But rather than

turning in for the day, you work on a proposal for a while, then finish up by checking your e-mail once last time. The next day you get up and do it all over again.

It's a crazy life, even a fragile life, where things such as traffic jams, computer problems, and sick kids can put you over the edge. There's no wiggle room in your schedule for you to learn new things and thus invest in your future. There's no mental bandwidth left for taking on anything else. It requires all of your energy to keep up with what needs to be done today.

You're not the only one who's feeling this way. Your customers are just as frazzled as you are.

They work in lean and mean organizations, consigned to sixty-plus-hour work weeks filled with endless meetings. The last thing they want to do is add one more item to their already overflowing to-do lists. Throw in an uncertain economy, and things get even crazier for these burnt-out people who are now expected to do even more with fewer resources.

Ironically, in this frenetic and high-speed environment, change can be unbearably slow. Your customers may spend hours online searching for answers to their most pressing problems, but when it comes down to the wire, they freeze and can't figure out what direction to take. Everyone has an opinion, no one wants to take a risk, and turf issues abound. Your customers are surrounded by complexity and chaos, and at the same time, they yearn for simplicity and order.

We've never faced tougher sales challenges.

Time for a Wake-Up Call

That's why I wrote this book. Because times have changed, and we must change, too. Because what worked before doesn't work anymore. Because the advice of many "traditional" sales gurus is now hopelessly outdated. And finally, because things are never going to go back to the way they used to be.

Yet in these challenging times lies great opportunity. Marketing legend Joe Sugarman once said, "Each problem has hidden in it an opportunity so powerful that it literally dwarfs the problem." I agree with him completely, and intend to show you where to find those opportunities!

Let me give you a bit of background so you know where I'm coming from. My own sales career began at Xerox Corporation, where I had great success in both sales and sales management. From there, I moved into technology sales, and in my first year was selected International Rookie of the Year. After that, I started a sales consultancy firm, helping companies shorten the time to revenue on their new product launches. I loved helping the sales force jump-start their sales.

But all that came to a screeching halt several years back when my two biggest clients simultaneously came under pressure from Wall Street. Forced to cut costs, they immediately chopped all unnecessary expenses. Consultants were the first thing to go! My business collapsed, and I had to start all over again.

What I learned in that comeback period was that everything was changing, and that if I wanted to be successful again I would have to change, too. Over these past few years, my perspective on sales has altered dramatically. In my first book, *Selling to Big Companies*, I shared some of the new strategies that work in today's business environment. In this book, I take it to the next level as I write about the fundamental shifts we all need to make in order to get in front of this rapidly changing marketplace. Some people won't like what I have to say. They don't want to change. They like their tried-and-true sales practices. In fact, right now they're probably saying, "We need to get back to the basics."

But this is not the "good old days" anymore, so I'm doing my darndest to be your wake-up call and bring you into the new reality. In the new sales climate, focusing on your FABs (features-advantages-benefits) creates insurmountable obstacles. Using clever objection-handling techniques insults your prospect's intelligence. And employing "always be closing" tactics is the surest way to prematurely end potentially fruitful relationships.

We're on the cusp of a new age in selling. It's a time to create *new* basics and let go of the old ones. For example, it's no longer a numbers game. You'll be much more successful making fewer high-quality calls, meetings, and presentations. And having a great relationship with your customers is nice, but no longer sufficient. Today you need to personally bring value to each interaction you have with these people. Also, even if you sell commodities, your new role in working with these well-educated customers is as a "business improvement specialist."

These are only a few of the many changes we need to make today. If you commit to learning these new basics, you will be unstoppable. And your competitors won't have a chance.

Crazy-Busy Decision Making

In this book you'll get an inside look at how your prospects actually make decisions—or don't—in today's crazy-busy organizations. Once you can see through their eyes, you'll be able to pre-evaluate your sales approach and refine it to increase its effectiveness.

First, you'll need to understand the three distinct decisions your prospects make before they sign a contract with you—or with your competitor. With the first decision, they evaluate your approach to determine if it's worth their time to meet with you. With the second decision, they determine if making the change will be worth all the disruption it will cause. And finally, with the third decision, their primary concern is selecting the best option for their company.

While we might hope that each prospect will turn into a customer, there are so many things that can derail, defer, or dry up even the best opportunities at any stage of your prospect's decision-making process. This is especially true when you're dealing with people who already have too much to do. That's why I've structured this book around each of these decisions. It'll enable you to isolate the problems you encounter and focus on the best strategies for addressing them.

In this book you'll be introduced to four new factors that need to be at the forefront of your mind when working with crazy-busy people. I call these the SNAP Factors:

Simple: Your ability to eliminate complexity and effort from your prospect's decision-making process will improve your chances for sales success.

iNvaluable: In a world of copycat products and services, the value you personally bring to the relationship becomes essential.

Aligned: You must stay relevant to your client at all times; they don't have time for anything else.

Priority: With an ever-changing business environment, you can't afford to have your prospect deem your services non-urgent.

Consciously or not, today's prospects evaluate you on these four criteria in every single interaction you have with them. If you dismiss the SNAP Factors, your sales efforts will become delayed or derailed. Worse yet, you don't always get second chances. Once you're dismissed, you're gone.

In this book you'll discover how to leverage these SNAP Factors across all three of your prospect's critical decision-making stages. Other sales training programs and books totally ignore the massive workloads and continual pressure faced by these people, yet these are the elephants in the room. Failure to address them puts your sales opportunity in serious peril.

Finally, in this book I've included ideas from many other top sellers and sales experts. Why? Because in a time of change, no one person has all the answers. The advice and stories from these savvy sellers with a wealth of experience add invaluable insights I know you'll appreciate.

What Sales Really Is

Before you dig in, I'd like to leave you with this thought: *Sales is an outcome, not a goal.* It's a function of doing numerous things right, starting from the moment you target a potential prospect until you finalize the deal.

So let's get started on this new sales adventure. I want you to see the possibilities in today's marketplace—even amid the incredible challenges—and discover how you can capitalize on them. Yes, it's a little bit scary, but with this book you're getting a blueprint of what you can do starting tomorrow. Start at the beginning so you lay a solid foundation. Knowing as much as you can about your targeted prospect is more important than your knowledge of your own product, service, or solution. Most sellers don't realize that, but it's true.

Once you know your buyer inside and out, you can easily start applying what you've learned to create customer-enticing value propositions, messaging, presentations, and proposals. Plus, this knowledge of your customer will be at the heart of all your best, most fruitful conversations.

Now that you're aligned with what they're trying to achieve and have focused on their top priorities, you'll start seeing a difference in your sales right away. Seriously. Then, when you start focusing on simplicity and personally bringing value, your business will really take off. I know you'll be pleasantly surprised.

This book will change how you feel about your job and make you more successful. Best of all, you won't have to work as hard as you do today to achieve significantly better results.

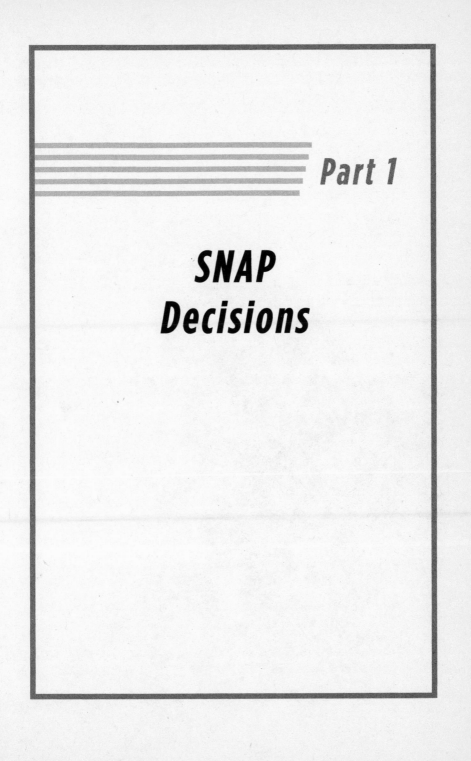

Part 1

SNAP
Decisions

1

It's Tough Out There

In today's crazy-busy world, reaching people on the phone is a virtual impossibility, as is finding a free spot in their already overfull calendars. Capturing and keeping their attention requires Herculean efforts. One day a prospect states their desire to change, but the next day they default to the status quo. Then, after announcing their intention to do business with you, they disappear into an impenetrable black hole of non-communication, making you wonder if it was all a figment of your imagination.

The good news is you're not losing it! The bad news? This is reality, and no one ever prepared us for a sales environment quite like this. You probably hoped customers cared about your offering. Maybe you thought they'd jump for joy when they heard about your company's capabilities or your passion for excellence.

Instead you hear them typing on their keyboard on the other

end of the phone or see them checking their BlackBerrys in the middle of your presentation. Overwhelmed and stressed, they don't think twice about being rude as they struggle valiantly to get way too much work done in way too little time.

How can they rationalize this unconscionable behavior? Let's hear directly from one of your prospective customers.

A Candid Letter from Your Customer

Dear Seller,

I have only a few minutes, but I understand you're interested in selling me something. As far as I'm concerned, that's pretty self-serving.

The truth is, you have no idea what my life is like. You may think you do, but you don't—and you need to if you're going to get my business.

I got to the office early this morning so I could have some uninterrupted time to work on a project—something I can't seem to squeeze into the normal business day.

By 9:00 a.m., all my good intentions were dashed when my boss asked me to drop everything in order to put together a head-count reduction plan. Revenue slumped last quarter, and we need to cut costs.

Then Engineering informed me that our new product won't be available for the upcoming trade show. Sales will go ballistic when they hear this. That's the last thing I need to have happen.

Get the picture? Welcome to my world of everyday chaos, where as hard as I try to make progress, I keep slipping further behind. Right now I have at least 59 hours of work piled on my desk. I have no idea when I'll get it all done.

Did I mention e-mail? I get over 150 each day. Then, add to that at least 30 phone calls from sellers just like you who'd "love to meet with me."

In short, I have way too much to do, ever-increasing expectations, impossible deadlines, and constant interruptions from people wanting my attention.

Time is my most precious commodity, and I protect it at all costs. I live with the status quo as long as I can—even if I'm not happy with it. Why? Because change creates more work and eats up my time.

Which gets us back to you. In your well-intentioned but misguided attempts to turn me into a customer, you fail woefully to capture and keep my attention. Let me be blunt: I don't care about your product, service, or solution.

I quickly scan your e-mails or letters looking for any self-promotional talk that glorifies your offering or your company. The minute it jumps out at me, you're gone. Zapped from my in-box or tossed into the trash can. Say it in your voice mail message, and I delete you immediately. Delete, delete, delete.

When you spend an entire meeting blathering about your unique methodologies, great technology, or extraordinary service, my mind wanders to important tasks that need to get done. Sure, I even occasionally check my BlackBerry for messages while you're speaking. But you would too if you were in my position.

I'm not always like this. Occasionally a savvy seller captures my attention, entices me to meet with them, shows me why I should change, and then makes it easy for me to work with them.

What are they doing? They're completely focused on my business and the impact they can have on it. That's what I care about—not their pitch.

If you focus on helping me achieve my objectives, I'll listen to you all day long. But you can't rope me in with the good stuff, then slip back into that trash talk. If so, you're gonzo.

Make sense? I hope so, because I'm late for a meeting, and while I've been writing this, the phone's been ringing off the hook.

Best regards,
Your Customer

Frazzled Customer Syndrome

While that letter from your prospective customer may seem brutal, it explains why you're struggling. The people you're calling on suffer from a severe case of Frazzled Customer Syndrome, a debilitating condition brought on by excessive workloads, 24/7 availability, information overload, lack of sleep, and job-related stress.

You likely encounter these individuals on a daily basis. They're good people who are doing their best to survive in a crazy-busy workplace. Their calendars are overflowing and they're constantly falling behind, but they feel powerless to stop the unrelenting, escalating demands on their time.

Their frantic pace is both exhausting and exhilarating. They can barely focus on important tasks because their days are filled with interruptions, distractions, and constantly changing activities. One minute they're working on a document. The next, they're checking e-mail, text-messaging, responding to a customer, or doing research online.

This frenetic multitasking fools them into thinking they're accomplishing a lot, but in reality they're doing very little. The result? More work, unmet obligations, unfinished projects, and chronic feelings of underachievement.

To make matters worse, they don't see an end in sight. Instead, they deal with constant downsizings and reorganizations and rapidly move from job to job, never really mastering their current one—all the while wondering if they're next on the chopping block.

Their personal life is just as frenetic, as they juggle work commitments, family, and personal time until they crash in front of the TV every evening. It's no wonder they don't have time for you.

Recognizing the Symptoms

How do you know when you're dealing with customers who suffer from Frazzled Customer Syndrome? Typically, they:

Have a "net it out" mentality. These impatient, time-starved people want you to get to the bottom line right away. If you don't, they're immediately dismissive.

Are easily distracted. Even when they're interested in what you have to say, their attention spans are short. They feel compelled to multitask whenever humanly possible.

Are forgetful. Because of their excessive flitting from task to task, much of what they commit to never makes it into their long-term memory.

Are demanding. They expect you to jump through hoops to fulfill their requests, yet when it's time for them to take action, they move like molasses.

Suffer from "analysis paralysis." Faced with lots of change, multiple acceptable options, and the lack of time for thorough research, they appear overwhelmed, and nothing makes sense to them.

Withdraw from contact. When they're buried under other priorities, they don't have any news to report or they have bad news, or they go silent altogether.

Frazzled Customer Syndrome makes your job so much harder. Dealing with overwhelmed people is completely different from working with calm, rational people who have time to analyze their situation and study multiple options before moving ahead. But those people are no longer the norm. To make matters worse, using traditional cold calling, presentation, and objection-handling sales techniques actually creates insurmountable obstacles that can derail your sales efforts.

Your hot prospects fizzle or flame out. They politely (or sometimes not so politely) tell you that their priorities have changed, the budget has dried up, or they have too much on their plate right now.

In most cases, your attempts to get them back on track are futile. They tell you to call back next month, but before long that becomes "next quarter," and then "next year." They just want to get rid of you. It's not personal. They just can't handle one more item on their to-do list.

2

How Frazzled Customers Think

What's really going on inside the minds of those frazzled customers that causes them to keep you at a distance, brush you off, dismiss you entirely, or stick with the status quo? Once you recognize how they think, and what you're doing that is bringing them to the breaking point, you can make changes to your own behavior.

Complexity grinds them to a screeching halt.

Overwhelmed people can't take in, sort through, or make sense of massive amounts of information, or multiple variables for a major change initiative. When they sense that the effort required will make their lives even more complicated, they call it quits—even if the change would have been good for them.

They subscribe to the "If it ain't broke, don't fix it" philosophy.

Busy decision makers don't have time for things that aren't urgent. They may limp along with all sorts of makeshift solutions and work-arounds. Their current way of doing things may even be draining massive amounts of money from their pocketbooks or their company. Even though it makes sense to change, they don't do it. It's too much work.

They think that making risky decisions is career-inhibiting.

Nothing is more off-putting to busy people than the thought of a risky decision that could turn into a quagmire, require additional effort for approval, or potentially put their careers at stake. Even a small whiff of risk is enough for many customers to decide to take no action or to do business with another company.

Most of their options seem like near-clones of one another.

Most products and services look pretty similar these days—especially to busy people. Even if you have a marketplace lead, customers believe it's only temporary and that competitors will soon catch up. When customers can't differentiate, they default to price as a key factor.

They suffer no fools.

In every conversation and interaction, frazzled customers are asking themselves, "Does she know what she's talking about? How much work has he done in this field? Is the company well known in my industry?" If they detect insecurity, knowledge gaps, or BS, they will want nothing to do with the seller or his company.

This shouldn't come as a shock. We all think like this when we're really swamped. It's a normal human reaction to a way-too-busy life, but it still makes selling tough. And in a challenging economy, this thinking is exacerbated as your prospects struggle with even greater workloads and fear of job loss.

When Too Much Is Too Much

Initially, I was stymied when dealing with people who were suffering from Frazzled Customer Syndrome. Yet a while back, when I found myself in their shoes, I began to behave the same way they did. My e-mail system had crashed, so any sellers who tried to set up meetings with me were brushed off as fast as I could say, "I'm not interested." I didn't act upon nagging problems because they took too much effort. Hot new projects came to a grinding halt, even though they were key to my business success. In retrospect, it is fascinating to note that many of my decisions weren't in my own economic or personal self-interest.

When frazzled customers slam on the brakes, you need to see this as a signal that you're currently on a crash course. Yes, it's painful when you've been counting on an order coming through. Yes, you want to scream when orders disappear into a black hole. And yes, losses to competitors who are "unworthy" (at least from your perspective) make you want to pull your hair out.

The truth is, we need to reframe these painful moments as

calls to action. Your sales success is in direct proportion to your willingness to see these struggles as learning opportunities—and then to dig in to figure out what works.

Descent into the D-Zone

Ever heard of the dreaded D-Zone? It's a place where prospective customers send sellers when they don't want to deal with them, want to avoid making a decision, or have no urgency to change now.

When you are in the D-Zone, your sales are Delayed temporarily or Derailed permanently, as customers Default to the status quo. You are Dismissed or Deleted. Your prospects Disappear or they're Dead to you completely.

In short, it's pretty depressing when you've been relegated to the D-Zone. When that happens, it's easy to blame your "idiotic" customers for making "stupid" decisions. You can also harp on how "rude" they've become. After all, "good" people would have the common decency to return your phone calls and meet their deadlines.

All this may be true. But when you think that way, you're missing the message. What you're doing isn't working. Period. You can blame everyone in the universe, refusing to see your role in being sent into the D-Zone. You can even feel superior to your customers, pointing out how they just don't get it.

But who's actually not getting it? Their decision to delete, delay, or dismiss you is their way of telling you that you need to do something differently. If you want to be successful in sales, you can't ignore this message.

It would be so easy to give up on frazzled customers. But if you did, you'd be making a big mistake. Remember, they're good people who are simply overwhelmed. They need help. They long for more time. They want better relationships. They're also striving to be successful.

They just don't have time to do a lot of thinking, so they make quick decisions about moving ahead or they slam on those brakes. Either you're in—and get a chance to move to the next step—or you're out. Game over.

Let's take a look at what you can do to increase your effectiveness with these people who could really use your help, even if they don't always know it.

3

Inside the SNAP Factors

Whenever frazzled customers deal with you, their brains immediately start firing off alert signals: "Warning. Pay attention." These crazy-busy people evaluate each interaction with you as they try to figure out what to do next. Should they invite you in or brush you off? Should they change from the status quo or stay where they are? Should they work with your company or chose a different option?

Every single phone call, e-mail, working session, demonstration, presentation, or negotiation is evaluated separately, within the context of the customer's current decision-making stage, and in relation to everything else that's currently going on in their lives. With all this swirling in their minds, here's what they're asking themselves about you or what you have to offer them:

- How simple is it? Will it take lots of time and effort?
- Does this person/company provide value?

- Is this aligned with what we're trying to accomplish?
- How big a priority is it? What's the urgency?

These questions are at the heart of the four SNAP Factors. Sometimes your prospects make lightning-quick yes/no decisions. Other times they seriously deliberate over their choices for months on end, and involve many people in the process.

It all comes down to a balancing act. There are only so many things your prospects can handle in their busy schedules. They have to stay focused on only those areas they feel will have the maximum impact—ones where the effort expended will give them the best returns. The projects that meet these needs are the ones that get the go-ahead. Everything else gets deferred until later or passed on entirely.

Your ability to stay in the Go Zone—where you're still a player and have a chance of getting the customer's business—is highly contingent on your ability to successfully leverage the SNAP Factors. But if you take your eyes off the Factors for even one customer interaction, you'll slip into the dreaded D-Zone and you'll lose your big chance. Let's take a look at each of the SNAP Factors in more depth.

SNAP Factor: Simple

Because of the state of overwhelm most customers live in, simplicity has recently emerged as a leading factor in sales success. Why?

Because people can't stand to add any more complexity to their lives. This is top of mind for your prospects. They are constantly weighing how much effort a new decision might require and where that decision falls on their internal simplicity-complexity scale. Notice how small the Go Zone is in the following simplicity-complexity continuum. Remember: even a small perceived complexity can be a tipping point, sending them into the D-Zone.

Most sellers rarely, if ever, take this into consideration when planning meetings, developing strategies, or interacting with prospective customers. Yet this failure to increase ease and minimize effort is a setup for sales derailment. You need to constantly monitor everything you do against this simplicity-complexity continuum. If something isn't easy or requires lots of effort, it's considered complex, and from a frazzled customer's perspective, that means it is:

Difficult to decipher

This can describe a wide range of flaws in selling strategies, such as <u>unclear messaging</u>, too <u>much information at once</u>, <u>inex-perienced customers</u>, or <u>buzz-word-laden presentations</u>. Many sellers are totally oblivious to how much they're confusing or overwhelming their prospects.

Difficult to decide upon

When lots of people are involved in the decision-making process or the amount of money being spent is high, the complexity of the decision grows exponentially. Competing agendas, confusion over direction, and disagreements can derail even the most beneficial decision for an organization. The need to explore multiple options to achieve the desired outcome further complicates things. And if there's any risk inherent in the decision, it muddies the waters even more.

Difficult to implement

It takes boatloads of time to work through issues and opinions related to initiatives that require revamping of entire systems, changing or eliminating people's jobs, or involving multiple business units or departments. When a decision is tough to implement, people are reticent about moving ahead with it.

You can tell you're complicating the decision-making process when you hear comments from your customers such as:

- "It gives me a headache just thinking about it."
- "Can you point out only what's really important?"
- "Are you sure your company can do something like that?"
- "I've reached my tipping point. I can't handle any more."

Also, it's human nature to tackle easier things first. They may not be critical, but at least they're doable—and that gives people a much-needed sense of accomplishment. Enterprise decisions or ones that span multiple divisions or departments are, by their very nature, messy and complicated. So it's no wonder people go that route only when they have to.

Remember, the greater the complexity, the longer the buying cycle and the higher the likelihood of losing to the status quo or to a competitor who made the decision easier.

SNAP Factor: iNvaluable

Even if you succeed in making things simple, you still must differentiate yourself. This is more difficult now than ever. Customers are fully cognizant of the plethora of perfectly adequate choices available to them. Even if your company is superior in any manner, they believe your lead will be short-lived and that competitors will quickly close the gap.

The only chance to truly differentiate yourself today lies in the value you personally bring to the relationship. And you can bet that your prospects are constantly assessing whether you're worth it. They truly want to work with smart, savvy people who bring them ideas, insights, and information they deem beneficial. Such sellers make it into their Go Zone, while sellers who fail to stand out on their invaluable-ordinary continuum get relegated to the D-Zone.

iNvaluable   Ordinary

GO Zone   ▲   D-Zone

What gets sellers thrown into the "ordinary" category? Frazzled customers have no time for sellers who have only a "skin deep" understanding of their world, use one-size-fits-all selling, or fire-hose them with a continual flow of information about their company or offering. You'll totally turn them off if you "wing it" or if you operate on cruise control. (They can tell—even though you think you're being smooth and charming.) Finally, if you're just waiting for them to give you directions about the next step, they've already written you off.

If even one of these statements describes you, customers will see you as dispensable. You won't stand out from the other sellers who call on them. You'll be doing just what they expect from sellers—which, quite frankly, is often very little.

Unfortunately, most sellers have no idea that customers assess the value that sellers personally bring to the relationship. And if you haven't invested in building your value, you have a high likelihood of being seen as ordinary—which for a frazzled customer is simply not good enough.

Remember, the less value you personally deliver, the more likely your customer will choose to work with another vendor who adds value, select a lower-priced competitor, or opt to stay with the status quo.

SNAP Factor: **Aligned**

The aligned-irrelevant continuum is the most important filter that frazzled customers use to determine who will be sent to the dreaded D-Zone. When sellers make the mistake of not clearly articulating how their product or service aligns with a customer's business objectives, they run the risk of being eliminated from consideration before they've even had a chance to demonstrate their true value.

Aligned   Irrelevant

GO Zone   ▲   D-Zone

As you'll see, at one end of the continuum is irrelevance. If you end up here, you and your product/services have been seen as extraneous or unrelated to the customer's needs. There is no in-between. In your prospect's mind, you're either aligned or not.

No one intentionally strives to be irrelevant. Yet if you ask customers why they dismiss most sellers today, this is the primary reason. Obviously there is a major disconnect between how sellers and customers assess this key SNAP Factor.

Prospects consider you to be irrelevant when you:

- Present information about your product, service, or solution before you understand their business directions and challenges.
- Use proof sources (case studies, testimonials, white papers) about customers whom the prospect perceives as fundamentally different from them.
- Share values and visions that aren't in synch with the prospect's corporate culture or what they personally believe is important.
- Know little about the prospect's business, industry, or market trends—but want to sell them something anyway.

Customers are quick to dismiss you the moment they detect an alignment gap. A telltale sign that this has occurred is when they say to you:

- "Thanks for sharing. We'll get back to you if we have a need."
- "We're already working with another company on that."
- "That wouldn't work too well here. We're different."

These reactions are difficult, if not impossible, to recover from. The only strategy that works is to avoid them altogether by being as tightly aligned with the prospect's needs as possible.

Remember, in the end, the less aligned you are with your customers' business direction, the less likely they are to want to work with you.

SNAP Factor: **Priority**

On a daily basis, frazzled customers are buffeted by newly arising emergencies, workplace reorganizations, shifting market dynamics, and ever-evolving corporate directives. They may start down one path, intent on changing from the status quo, only to alter their direction mid-stride when things suddenly change.

Urgent priorities will always be acted upon, but new priorities can pop into the Go Zone at any time. And when they do, your prospect shuffles things around on their priority-nicety continuum. With limited time available, something has to give. Previously important change initiatives thus slip into the D-Zone.

If at all possible, you don't want to get yourself in this position. If this happens, your prospects, who now have one more new item on their "must-do" list, will feel even greater angst and even more overwhelmed. And it will be even tougher for you to get on, and stay on, their radar screen. Because they don't have the mental bandwidth or available time to take action, they'll table any non-urgent decisions. And they may continue to compile information and lead you on in the hopes that they can "get around to it" in the not-too-distant future, but nothing ever seems to happen.

It's frustrating when you're trying to escape from the D-Zone but just can't seem to make yourself a priority. Many sellers, in their attempts to keep the momentum going, turn into professional check-in-ers: "I'm just touching base to see if something has changed?" That never works. When priorities change, everything changes.

> If you're not helping a customer with a high-priority issue or initiative, nothing's going to happen. If you can't keep the momentum going, your opportunity disappears.

We still live in a world where most sellers think they're selling products or services. But that's not true anymore. Your customers care about only how your offering adds value to their business and impacts their most important projects. And frazzled customers expect even more from you. If you don't give them what they want, you'll forever be relegated to the deadly D-Zone.

4

SNAP Rules: Simple + iNvaluable + Aligned + Priority

When you do figure out how to deal with frazzled customers, everything changes. They want to work with you. Sales cycles speed up. You have less competition. You'll be enjoying rich and rewarding collegial relationships, earning a good living, and making a difference—all at the same time.

How do you turn this into a reality? Just follow the SNAP Rules.

Rule 1: Keep It Simple

Your goal is to ensure maximum simplicity in everything you do. That's going to require you to look at all aspects of your customer interactions at each stage of the decision-making process to see where complexity can be eliminated or minimized.

You'll want to ask yourself and your colleagues:

- How can we simplify our messaging? Presentations? Proposals? Conversations?
- How can we make it easier for customers to understand the value they get from us?
- How can we help customers navigate through the decision-making process, avoiding the bumps along the way?

When you keep it simple, you make it easier for customers to buy from you.

Rule 2: Be iNvaluable

Today's crazy-busy customers want to work with sellers who "know their stuff" and bring them fresh ideas on a regular basis. Perhaps you've never even seen that as your role. But today it's essential to embrace the concept of being "iNvaluable" and turn yourself into the competitive differentiator.

Think about how you can become more knowledgeable about:

- What's important to the decision makers you interact with on a regular basis;
- Business processes surrounding your offering;
- What other companies are doing to solve similar problems or achieve similar goals; and
- Your industry—market trends, upcoming challenges, what's working and what's not.

When you become invaluable, customers choose you over competitors, are less price conscious, and remain loyal.

Rule 3: Always Align

Frazzled customers demand alignment. At the onset of your relationship, they need to see an immediate connection between what you do and what they're trying to achieve. As they move through their decision-making process, they need to know that the alignment extends beyond the product, service, or solution and into core beliefs they value in their business relationships.

To ensure alignment, you need to be able to answer these questions:

- How does my offering impact my customers' primary issues and objectives?
- What criteria are important to them as they make their decision?
- What do they value in their working relationships?

When you're aligned with critical business objectives, customers want to work with you.

Rule 4: Raise Priorities

It's an absolute imperative to work with frazzled customers on their priority projects. With their limited capacity, that's all they can currently focus on. To be in the Go Zone, target prospects whose priorities you can address, and focus on raising the priority level of initiatives that have dropped in importance to your prospects. Because customer priorities are constantly shifting, you need to be alert to what's going on with your customers.

Questions you can ask to stay out of the dreaded D-Zone include:

- What are your customer's current priority projects?
- How can you blend your offering's value into their priorities?
- What can you do to maintain momentum and increase the priority status?

When you raise priorities, your sales process goes much faster and you get the business with less competition.

Make the SNAP Rules your guiding mantra. Think of them every day and with every prospect. Integrate them into your planning and your customer interactions. Then, watch the positive impact on your business.

Doing a SNAP Check

To ensure that you're on track with the SNAP Rules, it's a good idea to get in the habit of doing regular SNAP Checks. While we've talked about each of the rules and factors individually, your customers evaluate them as a whole.

Even something as simple as a voice-mail message is evaluated on all four factors concurrently. Your product may provide exceptional value, but if your message is filled with gobbledygook, you'll be deleted. Or, you may have an easy solution to implement, but if there's no urgency on the part of the customer to act on it, your project will be delayed. Conversely, your service may have a huge impact on someone's business, but if it involves battling political agendas, your crazy-busy customer may decide it's too much work. Dismissed!

The sooner you can uncover any potential problems with a simple SNAP Check, the more time you have to take corrective action. Most important, you need to evaluate everything through the eyes of your prospects. It's their perception that counts, not yours.

If you were in your prospect's shoes, how would you rate yourself? To start with, look at the last voice-mail message you left or the last presentation you gave and place an X on each of the SNAP continuums exactly where you think your customer would put it. Be brutally honest.

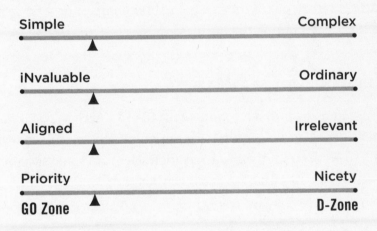

So are you in good shape—confident that your prospects see you as solidly aligned with their objectives and focused on a priority initiative? Do they perceive making a change as very doable without a ton of extra effort? And do they really want to work with you personally?

The SNAP Check simply shows how you're doing right now. If you're in the D-Zone, you have your work cut out for you. If you're in the Go Zone, you need to ensure you stay there.

You should realize that the criteria your customers use to evaluate simplicity, personal value, alignment with their objectives, and priorities will shift as they move through their decision-making cycle. The closer they get to making the final decision, the more they will scrutinize. This means you need to continually check how you're doing. Plus, different people will rate you differently. So don't forget to do a quick assessment of how each of the key players view you or your company as you move through the decision-making process. Again, you may find some shortcomings that can indicate to you what actions should be taken next.

Your goal is to have a strong awareness of where you currently stand so that you can be a solid competitor who has a great shot at winning the business.

When Should You Do a SNAP Check?

Once you realize what a good tool the SNAP Check is, you'll want to use it frequently to figure out your vulnerability and what you need to do to strengthen your position. Here are some situations in which you may find it particularly helpful:

For Pre-Call Planning

Before you contact a prospect, use the SNAP Check to determine how well your message will resonate. Before your actual meeting, use it to evaluate the likelihood of achieving your desired outcome. Anytime you use it as a planning tool, you significantly enhance your chances of success.

During a Meeting

Do quick mental checks to assess your status and then readjust your strategy as needed. Ask your customers pointed questions, such as "How challenging will it be to get your management team to buy into this decision?" Or make statements such as "This seems a little confusing," to elicit feedback. Knowing where you stand is a whole lot better than guessing.

When You're Stuck

When your customers go silent or don't seem to be making progress, it's a good time to do a SNAP Check. Something isn't quite right. If the decision were a priority for your customer, there'd be movement. If they felt there was value in your offering, there'd be movement. Anytime things are stalled, take a serious look at what you might do to get back in the Go Zone.

When the Decision-Making Process Changes

The day your customer decides that a change is necessary is the day they establish new criteria for their decision. We'll explain this in much more depth throughout the book.

After a Meeting

To flourish in sales, it's important to learn from your successes as well as your failures. If an opportunity disappears, use the SNAP Check to determine what caused it to do so, then brainstorm what you can do differently next time. If you win the business, use the SNAP Check to reinforce what you did well.

As you can see, a SNAP Check can be helpful in many different situations—all of which ultimately lead to more sales.

Remember, though, your customers—not you—decide if you're in the dreaded D-Zone or in the Go Zone. That's why you need to learn their thoughts and beliefs so you come to know them almost better than they know themselves.

To get the insight you need, spend time with your current customers. They're a great source of information and inspiration. The best ones for you to talk to are those who've decided to work with you in the last twelve months. Why? Because they remember the past, when they were working with other vendors, doing things themselves, or using other products. Ask your prospects, too. Since they want you to be focused on what's important to them, they'll gladly give you feedback.

Finally, you might want to do a customer immersion, an in-depth analysis of what's important to the various people who play key roles in the decision-making process. When you spend an extended time with your prospect, you can better understand their world. However, for many reasons, this is impractical. That's why I suggest gathering a group of colleagues together to complete an in-depth analysis of your targeted decision makers. When you can get inside your customer's head, you become unstoppable!

5

What's Going On Inside Your Customer's Head

D on't you wish you knew what your prospects were thinking? I can't tell you how many times I've written and rewritten phone scripts, letters, e-mails, and proposals, trying to find just the right words to get my prospects drooling, or restructured my presentations a hundred different ways to make them more tempting.

But all I ended up doing was confusing myself. With so many iterations to choose from, I had no idea which one would be most effective.

That is, until I discovered how to get inside my prospects' brains and think like they do. This ability to perform a "mind meld" enabled me to evaluate everything I was doing for its effectiveness before I was actually with my prospects. I didn't have to discover my mistakes during a meeting, where it is often difficult to make corrections. Instead, I could get it right the first time—because I knew what was important to my prospects.

You can do this, too. And you must, since your prospects' perception ultimately determines your sales success. It doesn't matter how well you think your meeting went, if you love your PowerPoint presentations, or if you feel your prospects could really benefit from what you're offering. The only thing that matters is how they feel about it.

Up until this point, I've focused on SNAP Factors, SNAP Rules, and the SNAP Check. Now we shift into application. From here on, you'll learn strategies you can use to keep you out of the dreaded D-Zone, strategies that will help your customers achieve what's important to them. When they win, you win!

Playing Brain Games

Knowledge of your product, service, or solution is simply a starting point. Yet that's what so many companies and sellers think is most important. It's not. Nothing, I repeat, nothing is more important than your customer knowledge. Without understanding your customers' business environment, challenges, and marketplace, you won't get selling right. And with frazzled customers, you won't get a second chance.

Over the past twenty years, I've worked with many sales organizations, entrepreneurs, consulting firms, and even individuals to help them learn how to think like their customers. In this chapter, you'll tackle the Buyer's Matrix—a tool I use to help sellers jumpstart new product or service sales, pursue different markets, call on C-level decision makers, and acquire new customers.

My clients tell me that this exercise alone is worth every penny they spend with me. Why? Because it profoundly changes how they approach selling. For the first time, they grasp why they keep running into the same showstopping obstacles, disinterested prospects, inertia, and the loss of customers to less worthy competitors. They also realize how their own behavior contributed to, if not entirely created, these problems.

On the positive side, with the Buyer's Matrix they see how they can make changes that fundamentally shift their prospects' perception of them and the value of their offering. They also discover how they can have a much greater and more positive impact on their customers' business.

Here are the steps you need to take to become effective at getting into your customers' heads:

STEP 1: Identify the Key Decision Makers.

What are the primary roles of the people involved in your customers' decisions today? If you're selling to corporate, government, education, or medical markets, you likely deal with a decision-making team. If you sell to smaller firms or consumers, only one or two people may be involved in the decision-making process, which makes your job a bit easier.

STEP 2: Complete a Buyer's Matrix.

After you identify the primary roles involved in the decision-making process, the next step is to complete a Buyer's Matrix (see pages 44–46, for each one. The word *matrix* means "the point from which something originates, takes form, or develops"—which is exactly why it's necessary to do this exercise first. It will provide the core foundation for your sales strategies. Plus, it will enable you to get inside your customers' heads so you can better serve their needs.

STEP 3: Create Customer Personas.

When you're done with your Buyer's Matrix, create several prototypical customers who represent the decision makers with whom you interact on a regular basis. In short, create a persona for each, which will make it easier for you to think like these people.

STEP 4: Use a Mind Meld.

Once you've created the customer personas, step into each person's mind to test all your ideas before implementing them. Using the SNAP Check, evaluate complexity, priorities, and personal and business value—as if you were your prospects.

Right now, this may sound a bit strange because nobody currently teaches this essential skill. Yet most top sellers do this intuitively. Because it's second nature to them, they can't even articulate what they're doing. But let me tell you, it's the simplest way to ensure that you're on track with your customers.

Profile Targeted Decision Makers

Completing the Buyer's Matrix can be a lot more challenging than you might think. If at all possible, make it a group exercise. Your combined expertise is far superior to your individual knowledge. You might want to consider involving the following:

- People with customer-interfacing jobs such as technical or customer support;

- Marketers who create tools, programs, and promotions to support your sales initiatives; and
- Your own leadership team, so you can get better insights into what's important to executives.

If you work for a smaller company, create your own team. Gather together a group of people who all sell to the same types of decision makers and start asking, "Who else might sell their products or services to [name of customer decision maker]?"

When you first use a Buyer's Matrix, you probably won't be able to fill it in completely. That's okay. The lines you leave blank will let you know what information you're missing and what you need to find out to be more effective in your job.

Each of the areas covered in the matrix gives you the essential information you need to better serve your prospects and increase your sales!

Involve your customers in this exercise. When you meet with them, explore the questions on the matrix form. If you're stuck, check with them for answers. When you're done, verify your results for accuracy. Remember, it all starts and ends with your customer!

The Buyer's Matrix

To help you see how it's done, I thought it would be helpful to complete a profile on my primary target decision maker, the vice-president of sales. If I want to sell my company's training services or speak at a company's annual sales meeting, this person must feel that I can help him achieve his objectives.

BUYER'S MATRIX

Vice-President of Sales

Roles/Responsibilities

What is he/she in charge of or expected to manage?

- Provides leadership to the entire field sales organization.
- Also responsible for inside sales, sales operations, and presales technical support.
- Drives sales of new products/services.

Business Objectives and Metrics

What does he/she want to achieve? How does he/she measure success? How is he/she evaluated?

The number one priority of the VP of Sales is revenue attainment—ensuring that the sales organization "meets the numbers." But in order to reach this goal, he/she focuses on key performance indicators (KPI), such as:

- Pipeline development: new prospects, presentations, proposals;
- Win rates: losses to competitors versus no decision;
- Percentage of team meeting quota;
- Percentage of repeat sales versus new customers; and
- Client penetration: amount of client's total available budget.

External Challenges

What external factors or industry trends might make it more difficult to reach his/her objectives?

- Competitive moves
- Rapid commoditization
- State of the economy
- Change in customer buying habits
- Longer sales cycles

Strategies and Initiatives

What likely strategies and initiatives are in place to help achieve his/her objectives?

- Implementing lead generation programs;
- Leveraging technology to speed up the sales cycle and increase sales productivity;
- Hiring top performers; upgrading skills of existing sales force; and
- Focusing on strategic alliances and channel development.

Internal Issues

What likely issues does the organization face that could prevent/hinder goal achievement?

- It's a struggle to get reps to use the CRM system and other new technology.
- There are delays in bringing new products to market.
- It's difficult to get a budget for training initiatives.
- Salespeople are unwilling to learn new strategies.
- There is a large turnover of key account managers.

Primary Interfaces

Who are the peers, subordinates, superiors, and outsiders with whom he/she frequently interacts?

- Regional sales managers
- Service/customer service
- Sales operations manager
- Vice-president of marketing
- CEO

Status Quo

What's his/her status quo relevant to your product, service, or solution?

- There is 40 percent sales force turnover.*
- Typically only 60 percent of sales force meets quota.*

- It is tougher for sellers to get into accounts.
- The average tenure is nineteen months for VP of Sales; fifteen months for sales manager.*
- There is some in-house sales training, most likely a form of consultative selling.
- He frequently uses internal subject matter experts for content needs.
- External resources are used for specialized training.
- Holds one annual sales meeting per year, plus multiple regional sessions.

Change Drivers

What would cause him/her to change from what is currently being done?

- She struggles to meet the numbers.
- He recognizes the skill gap due to changing marketplace, customer expectations.
- New customer acquisition is down; sales team doesn't even get invited to propose.
- Competitive losses are too high.

Change Inhibitors

What would cause him/her to stay with the status quo, even if they're not happy with it?

- There is poor success with other sales training programs.
- He/she is too busy trying to meet the numbers.
- Internal trainers see outsiders as a threat.
- Alternate uses of budget are deemed a higher priority.

* If applicable, use industry averages such as these.

As you can see, the completed Buyer's Matrix provides a rich source of information about the targeted decision maker. Once you really "know" your customers, it's much easier for you to:

- Develop customer-enticing messaging to get you into new accounts;
- Plan engaging meetings where you're discussing what really matters to them;
- Help your customers make the right decision for their business; and
- Differentiate yourself from competitors.

Remember, it's important to do a Buyer's Matrix for all your primary decision makers. If you sell to multiple industries, you may want to create separate profiles for various positions if their needs are substantially different. For example, the CFO of a growing technology company is very different from the CFO of a school district.

You can download a blank Buyer's Matrix at www.snap selling.com.

Now that you've completed a Buyer's Matrix for each of your primary decision makers, it's time to show you a high-impact way to use this information.

6

Your Customer's
Decision-Making Process

Years ago I attended a conference where Phillips, the electronics giant, presented a session on how they came up with their bestselling products. They'd created a prototypical family (mom, dad, and two kids) that represented their target market. Then they created a "fictitious" persona for each family member, complete with the person's age, education level, occupation, interests, beliefs, priorities, and daily schedule. Finally, to make them seem more real, they gave each person a name.

When the people at Phillips discussed new product ideas, they'd continually ask, "Would this be something Karl would like?" or "What are the biggest annoyances in Kristina's life?" In short, these personas became benchmarks to pretest ideas against before blindly running into production.

Shortly after that conference, I visited the vice-president of sales at a global medical devices company. Walking into his office, I was greeted by a life-size cardboard cutout of a physician standing in his white lab coat with a stethoscope draped around his neck.

When I asked about it, the VP replied, "He's our customer and we need to consider him in every decision we make. I'm always thinking about his needs, issues, and objectives."

Leverage Customer Personas

That same day, I created Bob, my first customer persona—or, as some might say, my "imaginary prospect." He guided my personal sales efforts for almost a decade. But then I noticed that in many companies, Bob was being replaced by younger, more aggressive vice-presidents of sales. So I created a new customer persona, whom I affectionately named Eric, after two of my customers at that time.

Let me tell you a little about Eric. He's a forty-two-year-old go-getter who's rapidly moved up the ranks in his career. In the past decade, he's worked for three different companies. He loves a challenge and throws himself into new jobs with vigor. He's been in his current position thirteen months and is working hard to achieve his ever-escalating revenue objectives.

Right now, he's under a ton of stress. The economy is taking its toll, and he's not sure how he's going to make the numbers. While he'd much prefer to take a long-term focus, he finds himself preoccupied with daily updates and short-term fixes. Competition is tough right now, and deep down he wonders if it's possible to meet his year-end goals. But he doesn't say this to anyone. Instead, he tells his sales managers to drive activity and find new customers.

While he is quite charming with customers, Eric can be abrupt when he deals with internal staff. He knows how much has to get done, and he doesn't want to waste a minute of his precious time. Because he's on the road frequently, he uses technology to keep in touch and on top of everything. The minute his plane lands, he whips out his BlackBerry to read messages, return calls, and check in with his family.

Eric is concerned that a couple of big accounts that were forecasted to close this quarter won't make it. Prospects are taking forever to make decisions these days, so he's constantly pushing his people to close the business (get orders, signed contracts, and commitments to go ahead). Some days he wonders if he'll ever have a breather. If Eric sounds familiar, it's because he wrote the letter in the first chapter of this book.

As you can see, Eric is very real for me. I could tell you a whole lot more about him, but you don't need all the details. What you need to do is to create your own Eric or Maria or Terry, so you can enter the mind of your customers.

Mastering the Mind Meld

Once you've completed the Buyer's Matrix and developed your customer persona, it's time to use this information to get you more business. Prior to making sales phone calls, I do a mind meld using "Eric." When I think I have a good script prepared, I call my own number and leave a message. Then I call myself back and listen as if I'm Eric. Usually I have changes to make.

I use a mind meld also prior to giving presentations. When I create PowerPoints, I review them from Eric's perspective. This ensures that they're focused on his business needs, not my company. Plus, it helps me catch all the acronyms or technical terms that may sound cool to me but are irrelevant to him.

In fact, I use Eric all the time. I develop questions based on uncovering Eric's objectives, issues, and initiatives. I develop strategies based on his short attention span. I create ideas to help him achieve his goals. My guiding question is: *What would Eric think?*

With Eric in the forefront of my mind at all times, I'm able to identify possible sticking points before they happen. This gives me a chance to make things better before my conversations with my real customers.

If you don't have one yet, it's time to develop this highly useful customer persona. Whoever she is, you'll find her perspectives truly invaluable in your planning process.

This may sound like a lot of work. Well, it is. But think about all the work you won't have to do because you're so much more effective in every customer interaction. That's the beauty of using this approach.

The Three Decisions

Now that you know what's important to your prospects, you need to take a look at their decision-making process. With a deeper understanding of how they think about change initiatives, you'll be better able to serve their business needs at the same time you increase your personal value to them.

Your prospects make three very different and distinct decisions in relationship to working with you. In some cases, you are the instigator of these decisions. In other cases, you're called in for a conversation after your prospects have spent considerable time researching their options.

First Decision: Allow Access.

At the onset of this decision, your prospects have minimal interest in connecting. Life is good—or at least not too bad. As you communicate with them, they will be evaluating your message to determine if it's worth it to have a more in-depth conversation with you.

Getting your foot in the door is your objective in the first decision. Your primary job is to initiate a conversation with the appropriate people. In order to be granted some of their precious time, you need to **move them from oblivious to curious**.

Second Decision: Initiate Change.

Helping your customers determine if making a change is "worth it" is the main focus of the second decision. The status quo is well imbedded in their organization, and any change that spans multiple work groups or business units comes with a whole slew of complications that already overloaded decision makers are loath to add to their workloads.

Getting conceptual buy-in to the value of a change initiative is a major first step, but it does not guarantee movement. Your prospects must feel confident that working with you is the best use of their time and resources. And because they rarely make these decisions, they need help figuring out how to do it. In short, your job is to **move them from complacent to committed to a change**.

Third Decision: **Select Resources.**

Your primary role in working with prospects at this stage of their decision-making cycle is to help them understand why working with you and your company is the best choice for them. After all, they can either work with you, do it themselves, use one of your competitors, or any combination of these options.

At this point, risk becomes a major factor—especially when the economy is in turmoil. There's still a strong pull toward the status quo. And your customers are evaluating which company they would feel most comfortable working with into the future. Your challenge is to **move them from being open to a wide variety of options to certain that you're the right resource.**

At each stage of your prospects' decision-making process, there are certain things you need to do to increase their interest in and commitment to change. If you do something at the wrong time—such as give product information too early—you will destroy the opportunity. That's why it's so important to know where your prospects are in the decision-making process. Your success depends on it.

That's what the remainder of this book focuses on. You'll discover which SNAP strategies work best to turn an initial phone call to a frazzled prospect into a meeting. You'll find out how to get that conceptual buy-in to change, and ultimately the firm decision to go ahead. Finally, you'll learn how to get crazy-busy prospects to choose you.

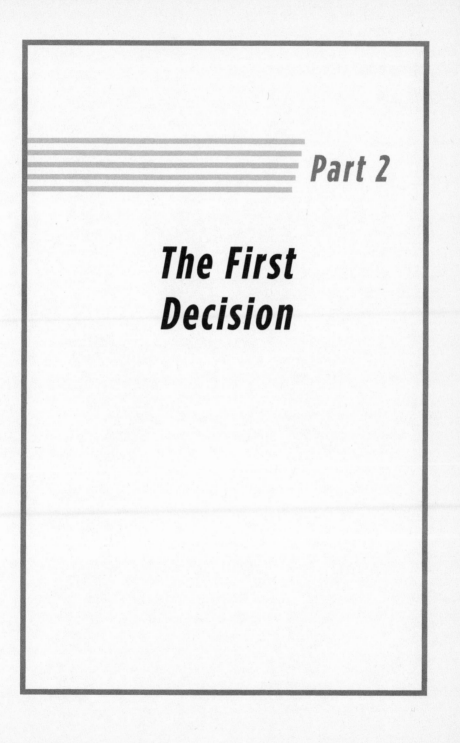

Part 2

The First Decision

7

First Decision Overview

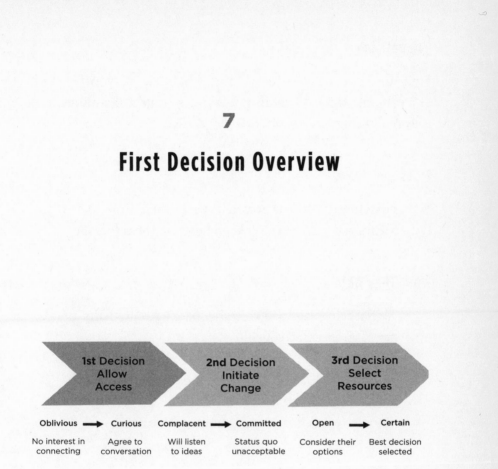

Customer's Perspective

Your prospects are busily going about their lives and their work with an already overloaded calendar. They're not waiting for your call. They're just trying to get done the things that have to be done. Here's what these frazzled customers are thinking:

- "I don't need any more interruptions."
- "I need to protect my time at all costs."
- "Salespeople are a waste of time."

Competition

Your primary competitor is any other use of your customers' valuable time: upcoming meetings, project deadlines, fires they're fighting, and their entire to-do list.

Risks and Fears

Your customers worry that you'll waste their time and, if they try to dismiss you, that you'll keep bugging them forever.

What They Hate

- Self-serving salespeople, passionate entrepreneurs, and process-obsessed consultants;
- Sellers who don't invest time researching their organization, issues, challenges, needs, or concerns prior to initiating contact; and
- Rookies who clearly don't know anything.

Seller's Role

Frazzled customers don't want to hear about your products or services. They will grant you access only if you pique their curiosity or provoke their thinking with relevant information such as:

- How other companies address the same issues;
- Business outcomes they'd like to achieve;

- Information on industry and competitive trends;
- Intelligence about their customers' wants, needs, trends;
- Updates on topics they're interested in knowing more about; or
- Insights into a vexing problem or new priority.

Big Challenge

To get a frazzled customer to grant you access, it's imperative that you convey all this information in a series of twenty- to thirty-second "touches" (via phone, e-mail, or direct mail). And if you don't do it right, you're immediately consigned to the dreaded D-Zone. On the positive side, your prospects' memories are so short that if you goof, you can reconnect again in another week or two!

Mission Accomplished

You'll know a prospect has decided in your favor on the first decision when they say, "Sounds interesting. Let's set up a time to talk/get together."

SNAP Considerations

Here's how the four SNAP Factors impact your prospect's first decision:

Simple

Once you understand your customers' needs, this is a key factor. It's critical to pack just the right information into thirty-second phone messages, ninety-word e-mails, or one-page letters.

iNvaluable

Your personal value will be assessed very quickly by what you say in your message. If you demonstrate an understanding of their business, objectives, and priorities, you'll differentiate yourself. If you give your "pitch," you'll be Ms. or Mr. Ordinary—a person not worth meeting.

Aligned

This is essential. If you are not aligned with your customers' needs, issues, or objectives you will not be granted access to the decision maker. Being ruthlessly relevant is the name of the game.

Priority

This is the trump card in the first decision. If you can tie the organization's or individual's priorities into your messaging, your odds of "getting in" will be increased exponentially.

Final Caveat

Most sellers don't pay nearly enough attention to the first decision. After all, from their perspective it involves just a short phone message or an e-mail that they quickly dash off. Because of this, they rarely gain access to the people with whom they want to meet—and they're constantly looking for new prospects to call.

In the next few chapters you will learn why:

There's no reason for this huge failure rate. You don't have to be perpetually consigned to the dreaded D-Zone.

It's best to follow explicit and detailed directions regarding getting your foot in the door.

The less time you have with someone, the more you need to ensure that it's time well spent.

8

Getting in the Game

Getting yourself invited into your prospect's world is the start of a relationship that may turn out to be incredibly beneficial to both parties. Unfortunately, many sellers never get their foot in the door because they're not focused on what's important to their customers. The worst thing is, they don't even know it.

Here's what you need to remember: Your prospects read your e-mails with their finger on the Delete key. They listen to your voice mails with their finger on the Delete key. And when your letters arrive, they may even be tossed into the wastebasket unopened.

Every three to five seconds during your initial outreach, your prospects ask themselves, "Is this of interest?" If not, you're gonzo. Delete, delete, delete. That's why it's so important to invest time in your up-front positioning and messaging.

We're going to start by looking at what doesn't work. Why? Because if you want to gain entry into your targeted accounts, you need to eliminate your sales-derailing, objection-creating behaviors from the get-go. Your prospects' BS detectors are on high alert. There's no room for error. The moment you're seen as irrelevant or self-serving, you're deleted.

Initially, this is going to feel brutal. You're going to discover all sorts of things you're doing that hurt your ability to gain access. But if you get deleted, you can't sell anything. That's why we're doing this purging and cleansing. By the end of this chapter, you'll be frustrated, because we're taking away all your best stuff. But don't worry. We'll ultimately replace it with what works!

Why Do These Messages Get Deleted?

Some are less-than-perfect initial contacts.

As you read the following messages to prospects, see if you can tell what's wrong with them, and try to do a mind meld with the frazzled customer on the receiving end of each message. And yes, they're all based on real examples, although the names have been changed to protect the guilty.

Voice mail to a VP of Sales

Hi, Simon. This is Jack from Great Sales Tools calling. At Great Sales Tools, we're the leading provider of powerful analytic solutions for SalesForce.com customers. I'd like to speak to you about a next-generation service we have called Sales Health Check.

Our customers are delighted with the new and improved visibility they get into their sales pipeline with this easy-to-use system. I'd like to set up a time to talk with you about the true power of these new capabilities and how they can be easily scaled for your company's needs. Please give me a call back at . . .

Would you have listened to Jack's entire message? If not, at which point would you have deleted him? When I work with salespeople, most of them get to "we're the leading provider of . . ." and call it quits right there. But there are other delete-producing terms in this voice mail: _next-generation, new and improved, easy-to-use, easily scaled_.

How would this voice-mail message rate if you did a SNAP Check? Because he is full of braggadocio, Jack is seen as just another irrelevant, product-pushing peddler. If he wants to be successful, he needs a whole new approach. Delete.

E-mail to the Company Leader

I'd like to introduce you to some innovative solutions designed to accelerate your company's growth. We're an industry leader in helping our clients address their most pressing business problems.

Our award-winning Strategic Partnership Services model helps our clients achieve their goals by giving them disciplined research and best-practice models to drive the implementation of cutting-edge growth strategies. By partnering with us today we can provide you with powerful benefits to your career and company, so now is the time to get started. We embrace a total commitment to helping you achieve your growth objectives.

I would love to talk to you and I am energized and focused
on making it happen now.

How long would it have taken you to delete this message?
If you're like most people, you make your decision within three
seconds. Most company leaders don't even make it that far in
this e-mail. Why? They don't want to learn about "innovative
solutions." End of story. They're too busy.

A SNAP Check would have immediately revealed that this
seller lacked alignment and relevance in the first few lines. While
the verbiage may sound impressive, it's actually just a bunch of
marketing buzzwords: *innovative solutions, industry leader,
strategic partnership, cutting-edge, powerful benefits*, and *energized*. Delete!

E-mail to the IT Department

My name is Melissa and I am conducting my periodic
check with you to see if we can assist with any of your
current IT/IS openings.

I work for Zero Consulting, a recruiting agency that
specializes exclusively in delivering highly qualified and
professional IT/IS consultants to companies in all
sectors and industries—some of which include the
Pharmaceuticals, Financial, Entertainment, Consulting,
Law, Healthcare, Banking, Manufacturing, Retail, and
Software industries.

In short, we offer one-stop shopping for all your IT/IS
needs. If we can help you in any way, we would be pleased
to do that.

Did you make it through the first sentence of this e-mail? Most people don't, even though Melissa is being really nice and checking back in. The laundry list of industries her agency works in—which was designed to show its broad base of expertise— only indicates to her prospects that she doesn't have a clue about their particular business.

A quick SNAP Check would reveal that Melissa is a big-time loser with no alignment, a mundane message, and no urgency. Plus, she needs to get rid of "one-stop shopping" thinking. Why in the world would customers trust a seller who obviously doesn't specialize in their industry? Delete!

Learn What Not to Say.

To make it easy for you, here's a list of words and expressions you need to eliminate from your vocabulary if you want to get your foot in the door. I know you like these words and probably use them all the time. But if you want to stay out of the dreaded D-Zone, they have to go!

Every seller in the world uses these fancy-schmancy super-latives and other impressive sounding words in the hopes of standing out from the crowd. Instead, they all sound like ped-dlers. Ugh! That's not what's intended, but it is the result.

Get Down to the Bare Essentials.

But wait! There's more! Delete-happy frazzled prospects want to deal with peers. Colleagues. Smart people. That's why you have to get rid of language that makes you sound like you're:

Pandering: Phrases such as "I'd be glad to meet at your earliest convenience" or "I'd be honored to meet with you"

Self-Promoting Puffery		
One-stop shopping	Impressive	Outstanding
Industry leader	Unique	Cost-effective
Breakthrough	Innovative	Experienced
Partnership/partner	State-of-the-art	Number one
Groundbreaking	Powerful	Premier
Technical Tripe		
Next-generation	Easy-to-use	Turnkey
Disruptive	Cutting-edge	Best-of-breed
Flexible	Value-added	Enterprise-class
Robust	Mission-critical	User-friendly
World-class	Leading-edge	Scalable
Creative Crap		
Outside the box	Strategic	Buzz
Innovative	Game changer	Make it pop
The big idea	Customer-centric	Break through the clutter
Synergy	Voice of the customer	Next level
Dramatic	Critical mass	Impactful

need to disappear. They put you in a one-down position, as do phrases such as "We're pleased to . . ." or "We're proud to . . ."

Passionate: Much as passion helps in sales, it doesn't help at the front end when you're trying to gain access. While you may truly be passionate, excited, or delighted about something, demonstrating that will sound like you're selling. And your prospect will say, "Whoopee for you, but why should I care?"

These phrases have to go because they're irrelevant and unbelievable. They reduce your credibility and get you deleted.

Plus, you personally become mundane, trite, and unnecessary. How painful!

Finally, get rid of all the how-tos in your messages. If I sent the following e-mail to a prospect who could desperately use my services, I guarantee you it would be deleted:

> My company offers a full range of sales training that starts with a complete assessment of your sales force's current skills. Then we do a gap analysis to analyze where they are today and where you want them to be. And finally, we craft a custom-designed program that will meet the needs of your salespeople in the upcoming years.

All this is overkill when you're just trying to get your foot in the door. It feels like way too much work to a frazzled prospect. Game over. Access denied!

Our purging and cleansing is now complete. You've been stripped of all those words and phrases that create objections to you and prevent you from setting up meetings with people who could be great prospects.

Don't worry. You won't be at a loss for words for too long. In the upcoming chapters, you'll learn what tempts and entices crazy-busy customers. You'll discover just what to say so that frazzled prospects will grant you access.

9

Aligned: Craft Winning
Value Propositions

et's start with the third, but probably most important SNAP Factor. Frazzled customers don't care about what you're selling. They're happily going about their lives, doing the best they can with the resources they have. While things may not be perfect, they're not horrid, either. They don't want to change anything, because for them, change is work.

To gain access, you need to create a gap between your prospects' status quo and what could be. Your targeted prospects need to see that there are options they don't know about yet—ones that may make their lives easier, save them money, or enable them to reach their impossible objectives.

At the onset of your relationship, this is all that matters. It's what wakes them up from their slumber and kicks them out of their comfort zone. You'll have a chance to "strut your stuff" later, when they're actually looking at making a change and want to know how you're different from your competitors. But not yet!

Alignment starts with having a strong value proposition that's highly attractive to your targeted customer—one that answers their question "Why should I consider changing from my status quo?"

A value proposition is a clear statement of the tangible results a customer gets from using your products or services. It's outcome-focused and stresses the business value of your offering.

Your strongest value propositions become the foundation of your foot-in-the-door campaign. They're also used in marketing and lead generation programs, Web site copy, collateral, proposals, and presentations. That's why I place so much emphasis on them.

When you get your value propositions figured out, everything else falls into place. Prospects pay attention. They can't send you into the dreaded D-Zone. What you're talking about is too important to ignore.

Ensure Front-End Alignment

Being able to clearly articulate your value—from your customers' perspective—is foundational to your sales success. If you don't have a value proposition yet, stop now and figure yours out. It helps you not only gain access to decision makers but also to understand the real benefit of what you sell. If you already have a value proposition, focus on fine-tuning it so that it's even more enticing to your prospects.

Unfortunately, there is no single "killer" value proposition that turns frazzled customers into begging buyers. Sorry. Different decision makers require different value propositions. Just one look at your completed Buyer's Matrix should show you that you'll need to emphasize different aspects of your value depending on whom you want to connect with. In fact, since you sell a variety of products and services, you could have multiple value propositions for each customer.

Value Proposition Generator

Over the years, I've worked with numerous organizations to help them clearly articulate their value propositions. And what I've discovered is that there's a formula for crafting a powerful one:

Value Proposition = Business Driver + Movement + Metrics

You'll need to include all these elements as you develop your value propositions.

STEP 1: Determine the Business Drivers.

Business drivers are what decision makers really care about. They are what the decision makers are expected to accomplish and how their performance is evaluated at the end of the day. In short, they're the language of business. As you customize your value propositions, pick out the business drivers that are most important to the person with whom you're working. Here are some examples to get you started:

lead conversion rate	•energy consumption	collections	downtime/uptime
cost of goods sold	compliance	labor costs	productivity
share of customer	operating costs	waste	turnaround time
customer retention	time to profitability	market share	time to market
lifetime customer value	profit margins	inventory turns	employee turnover
churn rates	acquisition integration	basket size	sales velocity

Make sure to identify the most important business drivers for the crazy-busy customers you're contacting.

STEP 2: State the Movement.

Customers won't change unless your offering is significantly better than their status quo. A strong value proposition always includes movement. Use words like these to help your customers realize the difference you can make.

increase	cut	improve	save	free up	revitalize
accelerate	reduce	enhance	squeeze	eliminate	shrink
strengthen	decrease	grow	balance	minimize	maximize

STEP 3: Add the Metrics.

Your prospects want to know how much you've improved something, the extent of the value realized, and how long it took to get those results. That's why adding metrics—or numbers—makes your value proposition even more enticing, powerful, and believable. Don't round your numbers, either—a 51.27 percent improvement is more believable than a 50 percent improvement. Metrics always strengthen your value propositions.

To get a one-page synopsis of the Value Proposition Generator, go to www.snapselling.com.

Real Value Propositions

Now that you know the value proposition components, let's take a look at some samples. Remember that when they're stated without reference to a particular customer, they should include the target market. This will ensure that potential prospects know for whom you provide these outcomes.

Web Marketing Firm: We help retailers increase their online sales conversion rates up to 58 percent and their average order size by 25 percent.

Document Management Company: We help distributors reduce their order-to-cash processing costs by an average of 67.2 percent at the same time they increase customer satisfaction.

Engineering Design Service: We help data centers reduce their power and cooling consumption from 13 to 79 percent.

Marketing Automation Firm: We help companies increase their lead conversion rates at the same time that they maximize their marketing spend.

Promotional Products Seller: I help safety departments slash accidents and significantly reduce their workers' compensation claims.

What's mine? I help sellers crack into big accounts and shorten sales cycles. Those are the primary areas I emphasize. But in order to gain access to prospective clients, I will often include specifics about a recent customer:

A leading media company was able to set up meetings with executives at 87 percent of targeted national accounts in just two months.

At a revenue management company, one seller landed a $5 million contract in only ninety days as compared to a typical sales cycle of nine to twelve months.

In just twelve months, a pre-press equipment firm launched a new product that achieved just under 50 percent market share in a marketplace dominated by one long-standing competitor.

As you can see, all these value propositions contain the three essential elements. They focus on business drivers that are important to prospective customers. The "movement" words show the impact on the status quo. And finally, the numbers add credibility and highlight the gap between what is and what could be.

Action Steps

Here are three things you can do right now to make your value proposition more appealing:

1. **Interview existing customers.** Start with newer customers—ones who have been using your offering for less than a year. They're most able to give you relevant, useful data in terms of how your product or service has impacted their business.

2. **Engage new customers in establishing metrics.** Don't be afraid to do this. If you're confident that you can make a difference, these numbers not only reinforce that confidence but also give you new results you can use.

3. **Review your Buyer's Matrixes.** Determine the primary value propositions for each of the major types of decision makers you call on. Next time you contact a similar person in another company, you'll be all set.

Finally, start using your value proposition in your phone calls, e-mails, and voice mails. It will help your customers know why it's worth their time to meet with you—and that's what you need in order to gain access.

10

Priorities: Capitalize on Trigger Events

While value propositions are the foundation of your sales initiatives, "trigger events" are the grand catalysts. They provide the context for irresistible messages to your targeted customers. Sellers who leverage trigger events outperform their colleagues and clobber their competitors.

A trigger event is an occurrence that shifts an organization's priorities. It could be internal or external to the organization. It doesn't matter. What does matter is that when it occurs, new objectives immediately gain importance, while others get tabled until things settle down.

Take a look at your own company to better understand what I mean. When you have a bad quarter, management wants salespeople to make more calls. When competitors introduce a new product, marketing immediately responds. When you get a new boss, he brings in his own ideas regarding the business direction.

Trigger events shake the status quo to its core. What was acceptable yesterday is no longer tolerable. New problems emerge that require resolution. Traditional vendors become vulnerable to shifting needs. Fresh strategic initiatives dominate the discussion.

What a perfect time for a savvy seller to get involved and help a frazzled customer. When you adopt a trigger-event mind-set, you:

- Gain access to decision makers in a nanosecond.
- Shorten your sales cycle significantly.
- Win business with minimal or no competition.
- Have contracts that are more profitable since you're not involved in pricing battles.

In short, selling becomes a whole lot easier when you're *aligned* with what's important in your prospect's organization and focused on a critical *priority*. These factors alone place you high on the SNAP check. All you need to do is create a series of simple but effective messages, and before you know it, you'll be in discussion with a hot prospect.

Types of Trigger Events

If you're new to trigger-event thinking, you may find it hard to conceive of all the opportunities that are available to you when one occurs. So I'll start out by showing you a number of different trigger events. As you review the list, ask yourself, "How might this event create an opportunity for our products or services?" (Note that this is not a yes/no question. It's a "how" question, purposely designed to get you thinking outside your normal thought patterns.) You might want to go through these trigger events with your colleagues to brainstorm their potential for your offering. Certainly not all will apply. The key is to find the ones that can have the highest likelihood of success for someone in your business.

Internal Trigger Events

These types of trigger events happen within an organization. Many you can read about in the business press or on your prospect's Web site. And for some trigger events, you need to know insiders to get the full scoop.

- Poor quarterly earnings
- A new strategic initiative
- Rapid growth
- An announcement of a new product
- Changes in ownership
- Venture capital funding
- Expansion into new market segments
- Opening up new geographies
- Real estate and construction activity
- Layoffs, downsizings, or rightsizings
- IPOs (initial public offerings)
- New relationships, affiliations, partnerships
- Mergers, acquisitions, or spin-offs
- Personnel openings in key positions
- The landing of a prestigious new client
- Lost customers
- Job openings
- Corporate relocations

Getting any ideas yet? One of my local clients, a copier company, keeps its eyes open for companies that are expanding, because they'll likely need more equipment. A leadership consultant I know watches for stagnant growth from firms in her market segment because she helps with turnarounds. A sales research specialist for several software firms regularly monitors job postings of targeted customers to see what types of projects the companies are starting and how his firm's services may help.

External Trigger Events

Here are some examples of trigger events that occur outside an organization but still have an immediate impact on the organization's priorities:

Dodd Frank

- Legislative changes: new laws, regulations
- Natural disasters
- Changes in the competitive landscape
- Changes with key customers
- Trends impacting the customer base
- New technologies
- Economic conditions
- Price of oil
- Cost/availability of borrowing money

Do any of these affect your business? When hurricanes hit southern Florida, a top sales rep for a company selling stored-value cards knew that retailers would need her product to ensure compliance with government regulations. An intellectual property attorney kept on top of legal cases relevant to his targeted accounts. When cases were settled, he used this information to initiate conversations with firms facing similar risks. When a savvy media sales rep heard that her primary competitor had announced a shortfall in earnings, she immediately contacted their customers in her territory.

Doors open wide for sellers who keep up-to-date on trigger events that are relevant to their sales success.

Determine Your Own Trigger Events

To home in on key trigger events, it's imperative to analyze your customer base. Listed here are three strategies you can use to identify those trigger events most relevant to your product, service, or solution:

1. Identify common goals, objectives, and strategic imperatives.

    In reviewing your best customers, it's highly likely you'll find that they were pursuing a direction that created opportunities for your offering. Perhaps they were focused on business drivers such as:

    • Entering new markets
    • Shrinking time-to-acquisition integration
    • Growing sales, revenue, or market share
    • Outsourcing nonessential functions
    • Improving operational efficiency
    • Streamlining the supply chain

2. Determine common challenges and issues.

    Another way to find your trigger events is to look at the issues your customers were struggling with prior to working with your company or purchasing your product. Perhaps they were facing issues such as:

- Declining profitability
- Ensuring compliance
- Increased competition
- Finding and keeping top talent
- Changes in customer requirements
- Inefficient processes and poor productivity

3. Review precipitating events on fast-moving customers.

Take a look at your customers who've taken action quickly versus those who dawdle forever when determining if they should make a change. Ask yourself questions such as "What happened inside their company that created or added to their sense of urgency?" "Was there something occurring in their external environment that caused them to suddenly take action?" If you don't know the answers, interview your customers. You might be surprised by what you learn.

Put Your Alert System on Autopilot

Many triggering events are newsworthy. Local, regional, and national newspapers carry stories about them. You'll also find info in trade publications and business journals, and on company Web sites.

But that's just too darn time-intensive in today's crazy-busy world. You can't afford to spend all that time sifting through hundreds of unrelated documents and Web pages to find those tidbits. Even if they can transform your sales results, it's still a lousy use of your time.

Here are some places where you can gather the sales intelligence you need to really take advantage of the opportunities that trigger events provide.

RSS Feeds

Many companies have an RSS feed on their Web sites, typically on the About or Investor Relations page. If you subscribe to it, you'll receive notification anytime the companies update their Web sites.

Google Alerts

Use Google Alerts to be notified when information is posted about targeted companies and/or your trigger events. You can receive updates as they occur, once a day, or weekly. This is a free service and can be very helpful. However, if you've signed up for lots of alerts, they can become quite cumbersome.

Subscription Services

In the past few years, companies such as InsideView and Dow Jones have launched alert services that monitor information from dozens of online resources and then alert subscribers. These Sales 2.0 tools find info on targeted companies, their executives, selected trigger events, and key company insights. Some can uncover hidden personal relationships through customers, previous employers, and existing customers. If you use a Customer Relationship Management (CRM) system to manage your prospects and customers, they integrate this information directly into it.

In my opinion, this is the best way to go. You pay an afford-able monthly fee to have all these capabilities. It frees up your time to act on this business intelligence rather than search for it. In short, it pays for itself in no time flat.

Imagine logging onto your computer tomorrow morning and discovering this headline: "Local Firm Lands $12 Million in Venture Funding." Then, in reading the article, you find that the money will be used in an area where your product or service would make a big difference. As you continue checking, you dis-cover that one of the people you need to get in touch with used to work at a company that's one of your best clients.

When these sales intelligence tools can deliver this much insight to us, it's definitely time to embrace them. Not only do you save yourself hours of time, you also get actionable information about the firm. You get timely alerts on the trigger events—enabling you to capitalize on emerging opportunities.

Trigger-event junkies truly dominate in today's market. That's because they pay attention to the SNAP Factor of Priority. If you can align your offering with what's urgent and immediate in a company, you change the whole dynamic of your initial con-tact with today's frazzled prospects. It's that big a deal.

When you find out about a trigger event, you need to act on it right away. It has an "expiration date"—meaning it's a hot pri-ority now, but by next week or next month, most of the issues arising from it will have already been addressed. So when the event happens, that's the time to get connected with prospective decision makers. This is when many sellers throw up their hands and say, "But I don't know anyone at that company!" That's what we'll tackle next.

11

Create the Critical Connections

I n today's turbulent economic environment, people are skittish about making decisions. They want to spread the risk—especially if it might cause disruption, cost lots of money, or have a big impact. So if you're selling to an organization, you'll likely be working with lots of decision makers.

Ready to get yourself in the game? You've already identified the job titles of your primary decision makers. That's a good start. It's important also to identify who works for, above, and alongside them.

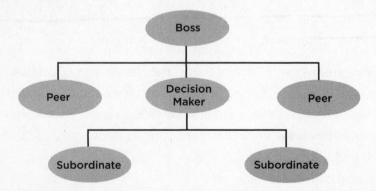

Every position you identify provides you with a potential entry point into the organization. That's good news. Your ability to gain access does not depend on the whims, preferences, or already overflowing calendar of one frazzled person. If you can't get your foot in one door, there are many other doors that could open for you.

Finding People's Names

Fortunately, finding people's names is a whole lot easier today than it used to be. The Internet is a veritable gold mine of information. You can either search for the decision maker's name on the Internet or use one of the excellent services available today. With these services, you can get individual names or buy a list that meets your very specific parameters.

There are three different data-gathering models out there today:

User-generated models: Jigsaw is perhaps the best example of this model. Their database is built and maintained by salespeople who buy and trade business contact information. You'll find hundreds of decision makers' names from small and midsize firms, and the names of mid-level decision makers at bigger companies.

Web-crawlers: ZoomInfo is a dominant player in this category. When you look for people in their database, you also find links to related articles, speeches, presentations, press releases, and more. Because they're so automated, these databases contain lots of good info from small and midsize businesses, too.

Human-compiled and/or -verified models: Dow Jones and Hoover's are several of the giants in this area, although there are many other well-known companies. They've typically focused on a company's senior executives. But now they're also leveraging the other models to increase the breadth and depth of their coverage.

Which is best? Ruth Stevens and Bernice Stevens, authors of *Online Sources of B-to-B Data*, recently conducted a comparative analysis of ten vendors to assess the quality, completeness, and accuracy of their data. According to them, it depends on what you're looking for. They recommend that you conduct a comparative test before you buy. One way to do that is to send each potential vendor a list of your house names and ask them to add data fields. Or you might order a sample of names and verify their accuracy by phone.

Also, check the Sales 2.0 section in the appendix of this book for a more detailed overview of the numerous tools that can help you find and nurture useful connections.

Leveraging LinkedIn

In the past few years, LinkedIn has developed into a rich resource for sellers. This interconnected network of professionals from more than two hundred countries is growing at the rate of over one million new members each month.

Because people create their own profiles, you can discover so much about them—including highly relevant information about their roles and responsibilities. Here's just one example from a LinkedIn profile:

Experienced marketer with a focus on Web strategies and "user experience." Job responsibilities include consulting with clients on online brand-building strategy; developing a professional sales and marketing department within a rapidly growing business; establishing sales and marketing processes; and management of sales, marketing, and creative personnel.

With this kind of information at your fingertips, it's easy to create messaging that's aligned with people's needs and key priorities. The guesswork is gone.

LinkedIn's search capability can be invaluable. You can search by title, company, school, location, industry, and numerous relevant key words. Make sure you use the advanced search at all times for the best results. However, if you have a free personal account, you're limited to seeing only the top one hundred searches. You must upgrade to a paid account to see more.

Business development specialist Leah Daniels finds that searching for people on LinkedIn is best done through Google. For example, if she were searching for marketing directors at Texas Instruments, she'd enter the following into Google search: site:linkedin.com "Texas Instruments" marketing director. You get more results that way.

There are so many other things you can do with LinkedIn that makes it such a fertile place for sellers. For example:

- Use LinkedIn as your home page. It keeps you up-to-date on what's happening to the people in your network.
- Anytime you get a business card, send the person an invitation to connect via LinkedIn. You immediately expand your network. And should your contact or you change jobs, you'll be able to reconnect later on.

- Most LinkedIn members choose to "show" their connections. Look for mutual first- and second-degree connections who can make introductions for you.
- While you're looking at a profile, check out the "Viewers of this profile also viewed" sidebar to discover other people who may work closely with this individual.
- To identify more relationships within companies, take a look at who recommended the LinkedIn members whose profiles you're checking and whom they recommend.
- When you search by company name, you get a list of all past employees who have LinkedIn profiles and their relationship to you. You can also uncover new hires, former employees, recent promotions, and much more.

Real LinkedIn Success Stories

Since most people are grossly underutilizing LinkedIn's capabilities, I thought you'd find it helpful to see how your peers are leveraging it to make connections and win business.

Making direct connections to prospective customers.
When Silvia Quintanilla, president of Industry Gems, wanted to get into a technology company, she identified and then e-mailed a well-crafted message to the director of Financial Services. He responded that he was leaving, but gave her his replacement's contact info. She landed an appointment that quickly led to an initial $60,000 project, which is fairly sizable for her business.

Using common bonds to open the door.
When national account executive Jack Conway wants to get into a new company, he leverages preexisting bonds with people

such as college alums and the "fraternity" of salespeople. Once when he was stymied in his efforts to meet with the CFO, Jack searched LinkedIn until he found a top salesman from the company. He sent him a message in which he appealed to their common bond, explained his challenge, and briefly laid out the business case. Jack said, "After the sales guy checked me out online and even interviewed me, he then set the stage for me to call directly to the CFO. I landed an appointment right away."

One good deed deserves another.

After Mary Anne Doggett, managing partner of Interactive Communications, spoke at a conference, she received a LinkedIn invitation to connect with an unemployed attendee. Because of his strong credentials, she offered to keep her eyes open for him. Shortly after, he announced that he'd landed a job—at one of her targeted accounts. She wrote back, congratulated him, and asked for assistance. Because of her willingness to help him, he sent her invaluable information on the company's key contacts and competition. She landed an appointment immediately. Mary Anne adds, "The basic premise of LinkedIn is that it appeals to people's need to help—even strangers!"

Online Networking Success

While LinkedIn is the giant for business-to-business (B2B) sellers, Facebook is the fastest-growing social media networking site. From a sales perspective, its focus is more on the consumer market, for people who are selling to individuals or smaller businesses. Companies are now able to set up "fan" pages for people who love their "stuff" and want to be connected.

There are many other online communities that are excellent

for networking. A few that come to mind are BizNik, Perfect Networker, and the Greenlight Community, all of which are rapidly growing right now. Here's how B2B sellers are using these online networking resources.

Reconnecting with old friends.

Software account executive Mark Secko started using online networking to get in touch with high-school friends, but he reverted to using it for business when he reached out to an old buddy who was a partner in a design firm. In an e-mail, he asked how his old pal was handling the financials. Since he was already a friend, he got an honest answer, to which he responded with several options. As Mark says, "Facebook works if you have a relationship with the person, and they trust and know you."

Turning online contacts into real ones.

Before heading off to a national convention, comic book expert Michael LoSasso and his wife, Tina, made a list of all the Facebook friends he wanted to connect with. When they got to the convention, they made the rounds, had a great time, and established lots of important relationships. After the event, Tina said, "The younger generation uses Facebook to keep in touch with people they already know. The older generation uses it to find people they want to meet."

From discussion boards to serious discussions.

Business consultant Rick Venet is a prolific user of multiple online professional and social networking sites. He's leveraged these methods for years with clients, to gain valuable information (both organizational and personal), obtain introductions with key personnel, and secure meetings with potential prospects.

Beyond LinkedIn, he's found that ExecuNet's discussion boards have resulted in phone calls about business opportunities. Using SalesNet, he's identified key contacts in an account.

Turning tweets into meets.

Trevor Lever sells contact management software. He monitors Twitter for specific key words that indicate competitive problems. When he identifies tweets such as "Once again, XXX has crashed" or "Struggling to install the latest version of YYY," he sees these as potentially hot opportunities. "But I tweet back, offering help," says Trevor. "The more I offer free advice to these stressed-out people, the better chance I have of getting a meeting."

Now that we know it's not so difficult to find these connections, our key challenge is to create the message that cannot be ignored. Fortunately, because so much information is available online about your future customers, you'll have a better chance of ensuring alignment with their key business initiatives and top priorities.

12

Simple: Messages That Matter

I f you're like most sellers, you're probably skeptical that changing your message could make a big difference. After all, you've
tried different approaches over the years and are still having
trouble setting up meetings. Much as you hate it, it seems that
making more calls and leaving more messages is your only option.

The good news is you're wrong. It doesn't have to be that way.
For example, how would you like to:

- Send an e-mail to a targeted CEO and within eight
  minutes get a return message requesting more
  information?
- Place your first call to a vice-president on Friday afternoon
  and get a call back from this person on Saturday morning?

Do I have your attention yet? I sure hope so, because these
are real-life examples from two skeptics who, out of sheer

frustration, finally decided to try my strategies. They were so stunned with the results that they e-mailed me immediately.

I've also heard from sellers who've embraced this prospecting methodology and seen dramatic results over time. One business consultant told me that once she started using these strategies, her sales increased 30 percent over two years. And after failing miserably the previous year even though he'd made more than 2,500 phone calls, a printing sales rep generated over $1 million in net new business.

In this chapter, we're going to start pulling all of these strategies together to show you what it takes to set up meetings with people who can buy your products and services. It's not hard, but it does require up-front work.

But first, the big question . . .

Voice Mail or E-mail: Which Is Best?

When I wrote *Selling to Big Companies* a few years ago, many sellers weren't sure if it was right to use e-mail to connect with "strangers." They didn't want to be seen as spammers or uninvited guests in a prospect's in-box.

While some people still feel this way, the use of e-mail prospecting has blossomed. For many of your prospects, it's the preferred method of communication. There are a lot of reasons for this:

- It's faster to read a message than to listen to a lengthy voice mail.
- It enables you to select the sequence in which e-mails are read.

- It requires less effort to give a quick e-response.
- It's much easier to delete or dismiss a seller online than in person.

In fact, many people today don't even listen to their voice-mail messages for days—if at all. Recently you've probably encountered messages such as "I'm sorry. The voice-mail box of the person you're trying to reach is full."

Younger people and those who work in the technology field are the most likely to dislike voice mail. They see it as a dated technology that's well past its prime. But they're not the only ones. This feeling is rapidly spreading to frazzled customers everywhere.

Some people now have messages that state, "I check my voice mail once a week. If you want to reach me immediately, use my e-mail." Others use services that translate voice-mail messages into e-mail so they can have the flexibility and speed they want. This is a trend that will continue to grow in the upcoming years.

So which is better? The answer is simple—whatever the person you want to connect with prefers. Some people still prefer the phone and always will. Others will only communicate via e-mail.

When you don't know preferences, your best bet is to combine both approaches. Leave a voice mail and mention that they can expect an e-mail from you shortly. Send an e-mail and let the person know you'll be trying to reach them by phone at a specific time. Never rely on just one or the other until you know for sure.

Paying the Price of Admission

To become an invited guest into your prospects' world, there are some things you must do. Period. There are no shortcuts. Frazzled prospects expect you to do this prior to initiating contact. Failure to do so will nearly always consign you to the dreaded D-Zone.

- If you're calling on a medium-size or larger company, you need to have researched their business. You're expected to have visited their Web site and learned about their direction, challenges, issues, and concerns.
- If you're calling on smaller companies, you can't invest time learning about each one. They don't expect that. However, they do want you to know about similar businesses in their market space.
- If you're calling on individuals, you need to know about people like them. For example, older people have different interests and concerns than families with small children.

Your prospects are just too busy these days to waste their time with you if you don't pay this price of admission.

Crafting the Message That Cannot Be Ignored

We all want a message so irresistible that sellers immediately pick up the phone to call you back. And it truly is possible for that to happen. Here's the proven formula, which I detail in *Sell-*

ing to Big Companies. It works for both voice-mail and e-mail messages—with only slight variations.

1. Establish Credibility

To capture the attention of a frazzled person, it's imperative to immediately establish your credibility. You need to be taken seriously from the get-go. Here are three suggested ways to do this:

- **Reference a referral.** If you have one, this is the ultimate way to ensure you're heard. Please note that having a referral alone is insufficient to get time on a busy person's calendar.
- **Cite your pre-call research.** This demonstrates that you've paid that "price of admission." Show your prospects that you've invested time on them prior to calling.
- **Mention a trigger event.** Again, this shows you've paid the "price of admission" and are up-to-speed on what's happening in their company.

Doing this sets you apart from 95 percent of other sellers who are trying to reach this crazy-busy person. He or she will keep listening.

2. Pique Curiosity

After reviewing what you know about your targeted company and what's important to your prospective customer, determine what would pique their interest the most.

- **Communicate your value proposition.** Make sure it's aligned with important business drivers and includes movement from the status quo and, if possible, metrics.

- **Share an insightful idea.** Good ideas are highly enticing to crazy-busy customers. They're too busy fighting fires to look ahead, so they need your insights.
- **Allude to important information.** People are always interested in market trends, their customers, and how people solve similar problems or achieve similar goals.

If you're talking like this, they will have to keep listening. Your message is so aligned with their business issues and goals that they can't delete it.

3. Close for Next Step

Voice-mail messages should end with the quiet confidence of a peer, with your follow-up clearly stated: "Let's set up a time to talk about this. I'll give you a call tomorrow to see if we can get something on the calendar." E-mails need to close differently. They should invite the recipient to engage with you on a non-threatening next step. "Here's the link to an article on how we helped Generic Systems with that issue. You might want to check it out. I'll follow up in a couple days to answer your questions."

This is the format that gets those great responses you read about at the beginning of this chapter. You need to customize it based on whom you're calling. If you're calling plant managers of small manufacturing firms, your message will likely be the same for all of them. However, if you're trying to set up a meeting with a big company and have lots of upside potential, the people you're trying to reach should know unequivocally that this message is only for them.

You might also want to try what Michael Boylan, author of *The Power to Get In,* recommends. He's had incredible success launching account entry campaigns targeted at the primary decision maker, her boss, several peers, and a couple of underlings. Each person gets the same business-case-focused letter on the same day. And each is informed that others have received the same letter. This gets them all talking about who should be meeting with you—and voilà! Someone gets assigned the responsibility.

Radical Sales Makeovers Work

Alex, a senior sales executive, began his career in the technology field during its heyday. To set up meetings, it was common practice to hype the company's leading-edge, robust, scalable systems in the messages. Much as he loved building relationships with clients, Alex knew that it would happen only after he'd made endless prospecting calls.

When he took over a new job in the medical field, he immediately started dialing for dollars and blasting his territory with promotional e-mails. After a few months, he had zero results to show for his work. That's when he decided to start using the "messages that can't be ignored" format. After working hard to craft an enticing voice mail, he finally made his first call:

Tom, this is Alex with Medical Marketing Applications. Lisa in your Tampa office said I should talk with you. I saw on your Web site that you're the "newest" division of the company and plan to expand into the U.S. market.

In working with other medical device manufacturers,
we've helped them decrease the lag time between product
launch and reaching forecasted sales goals. We should get
together and talk about how we can reduce the amount
of time you're spending on the road this year, too. I'm
available after 1:00 pm today at . . .

[handwritten margin notes: reference, Business Driver, Value Prop.]

When he got back from lunch, Tom had called back, talked briefly with the officer manager, left his e-mail address, and requested more information—even after saying he wasn't interested. Alex followed up via e-mail.

Thanks for returning my call today. Sarah said you don't
have any pressing needs right now but still wanted some
info. I'll send you a CD that includes some projects we've
created for medical device firms such as [he included a
list of three well-known companies].

In a nutshell, they were spending lots of money with each
new product launch to train their sales organizations,
physicians, clinicians, and patients. How much money
can be saved with effective sales tools? A leading
orthopedic device manufacturer recently reduced field
travel by 40 percent.

Please send your address so I can mail you the CD. Call
me and we can talk about what your challenges are,
and how I can assist you. Bottom line: we need
to make sure that your organization is accelerating
time to profitability while reducing labor costs at
launch time.

Remember, he sent this e-mail to a prospect who already said he wasn't interested. But look at how his prospect responded:

> Thanks for your interest in our company. I visited your Web site today and am excited about the possibilities. We're very much in start-up mode right now, balancing a plethora of needs as we ramp our business. Your solutions could be right around the corner for us. As requested, my contact info follows.

Alex immediately followed up with him via e-mail:

> I'll send out a CD today. I completely understand "start-up mode," as I've been involved in them myself. I appreciate how many hours you're putting in. And of course, everyone wants to know "how many units did we sell today?"
>
> Over the past week, I spent a lot of time reviewing your Web site. It appears that one of the primary goals is to provide your customers with detailed knowledge about how your products actually work.
>
> I have some ideas about how we might provide this information in a way that can help your sales team reduce training time, while increasing learning retention. Take a look at the CD I'm sending. Then let's set up a time to talk in more detail about how we can help you ramp up and exceed quota.

His frazzled prospect got right back to him with this next e-mail:

You've nailed our situation on the head. Start-ups are always challenging. Although we're a global competitor, in the U.S. we have relatively low name-recognition. We've built a network of 170 independent distributors who focus on our target market.

After reviewing your materials, we can talk more about your specific applications and possible opportunities. Looking forward to getting together soon.

Why This Makeover Worked

Let's take a look at the SNAP Factors to better understand why Alex's messages were so successful.

- **Simple:** They cut through all the clutter. They were short and to the point.
- **iNvaluable:** He stood out from other sellers because he'd done his homework prior to making the call. He knew about the challenges facing start-ups and he offered only ideas.
- **Aligned:** In his messages, he focused on key business drivers such as decreasing lag time on product launch, reduction of travel expense and training time, ramping up sales, exceeding quota, accelerating time to profitability, and reducing labor costs.
- **Priority:** He identified two trigger events: new product launches and the expansion into the U.S. market.

And as you can see, Alex created messages that could not be ignored. That's what this approach is all about. It's subtle. It's simple. It's helpful. It's personable. It's informative. It's relevant and it's even urgent. And he resisted that temptation to make a pitch for his company's services. That's why it works.

Best of all, he doesn't have to make a million phone calls. Alex is maximizing his own time because he's targeted opportunities where he has a good chance of being successful. And then he's ensuring that his messages matter to prospective customers.

Do you see how this type of messaging will fundamentally change the conversation in your initial meeting? You won't be talking products or services—because that's not what your prospects are interested in. Your conversation will be about their business, needs, issues, and challenges. While you may not feel like you're "selling," you're actually making more progress in your sales efforts than before. By not selling, you're actually further ahead because now you're talking to someone who really wants to listen to you.

13

Passing the "Tell Me More" Test

Once you've learned to create those customer-enticing messages, two things will happen: (1) When you reach a human being on the phone, they'll be interested, and (2) decision makers will call you back to learn more. How you handle these opportunities is vital to your sales success.

Recently I did a training session for an event management company. Like everyone, they struggle to gain access to frazzled customers. We fine-tuned their value proposition and then tackled their messaging. From my perspective, everything looked pretty good. I could easily envision their customers being really interested in what they were doing. I was confident they'd gain access.

That's when Scott raised his hand. "Jill, that's pretty much what I always say when I contact people," he said. "But I still have problems setting up meetings when I get them on the phone."

The Bitter Truth Comes Out

Mmmm. I was stumped at first. Then I said, "Let's do a little role-playing. I'll be your customer." Since we'd spent part of the morning on the Buyer's Matrix, I knew what was important to this decision maker. It was easy for me to get into the mind meld.

I picked up the imaginary phone and said, "This is Jill." With that, Scott delivered an impeccable message. As his customer, he hit on the key points that were most relevant to my business today. Then he tied it all together with his knowledge of what was happening in my company at that moment. It was really good.

"That's really interesting, Scott." I said. "Tell me more."

"I'd be glad to," he answered. "Our company has been in business since 1997. It was formed by four separate firms— each with its own expertise in the communications field. They came together to address the greater challenges faced by global companies today. Since our merger, we've been growing at the rate of 28 percent annually, now making us the leading provider of these services in the country. We offer a full range of services for all your marketing and communications needs including . . ."

After his second sentence, I'd checked out. He'd just flunked my internal "tell me more" test by reverting back to that same gobbledygook that turns customers off from the beginning. Nothing he said was aligned with my business objectives or priorities. It was a bunch of self-serving information that was totally irrelevant to me as a prospect.

Poor Scott. He was just about to gain access, but he lost it.

He descended into the dreaded D-Zone, and as his customer, I wasn't going to let him out. Very politely, I said, "Thanks, Scott. It's interesting what your company does. Why don't you give me a call back in six months? We might have something then."

Do you see how easily that happened? Scott had no idea that his explanation was a problem. In fact, it was a good recitation about his company and its growth, but that's not what his customers wanted to know.

What Customers Are Really Asking

Okay. Now you're confused. What are you supposed to say when prospects want more information about your company, product, or service? After all, they asked for more, and I'm telling you not to give it to them.

When you're in the early stages of working with prospective customers, the answer to "Tell me more" is not a company overview. Nor is it a description of your process or methodology. It isn't a request for more in-depth information about your products, either.

Remember, you're talking to people who suffer from Frazzled Customer Syndrome. Do you think they care about all that?

So what do your prospects mean when they say, "Tell me more"? If you shared a strong value proposition or customer metrics, they want to know how you achieved those business outcomes. And they're not interested in hearing about it in excruciating detail.

When you respond to them, it's important to demonstrate your knowledge of their business issues and let them know the high-value results you can deliver. To pass the "Tell Me More" test, follow these guidelines:

1. Expand on the issue.

Since you started out by stating you could help companies address specific issues or challenges, expand on that first. Talk about how tough it is for companies to achieve their objectives using outdated systems or processes. Talk about the difficulties that arise, the bottlenecks, work-arounds, and frustrations. Mention the ramifications of these for other areas in their business.

2. Share a success story.

Let your prospect know about a particular customer you recently worked with, how they were doing things when you initially started working together, the problems they faced, and the impact of these problems on their business. Then briefly summarize the outcomes.

Warning! Do not get into a sales pitch for your offering. Say, "while using our system" or "during the course of our project" or "the new technology enabled them to." But that's as deep as you want to go—even if they ask more questions.

You may need to have several stories for different types of organizations you call on. And depending on whom you're talking to, your story may have an entirely different emphasis. Refer to the Buyer's Matrix to stress what's really important to your particular prospect.

3. Engage your prospect. Ask a question of them

Never tell your success story and then just wait for a response. Instead, wrap it up by asking a question that engages your prospect in discussing the issue in greater depth. This helps the people you're talking to connect what you've just shared with their personal situation.

If they're interested, don't stay on the phone long. Your goal is to set up a meeting. Simply state that the purpose of your call was to set up a time to talk, not to have a conversation right now. Then offer several dates and times that work for your schedule.

These guidelines virtually guarantee that you'll stay in Go Zone. Your success story was aligned with their business needs. It was about a priority issue. And it demonstrated your personal expertise, thus making you more valuable to your prospect.

Tighten Your Story

Always remember the first SNAP Rule: Keep it simple! When you're sharing your success story, it's natural to go into too much depth. Some people start rambling and can't stop. You don't have that much time—maybe sixty seconds, max.

Think about the most important points of your story—from your customer's perspective, not yours. Then practice telling your story out loud. Do it a couple times until you feel that you can easily respond to the "Tell Me More" request.

Next, record your story. Call your own voice mail and tell your story there. Use your cell phone if it has that capability. Tape it, time it, and listen to it in mind-meld mode. You need to get rid of all the blather that weakens your story.

Here's an example. It's my "Tell Me More" response to a VP of Sales. As my business has changed, so has the success story I tell. But this is what I've found really resonates for my decision maker today:

Tell me More...

Expand

In virtually every B2B sales organization we talk to today, new customer acquisition is a key strategic imperative. Frazzled customers don't want to meet with salespeople. They're deleting their voice mails and e-mails as fast as they come in. (*Expand on the Issue*)

Story

Recently we did a project with a large media company that was targeting national advertisers. Prior to the session, each salesperson researched a targeted account they wanted to land as a client. In many cases, they'd been trying unsuccessfully to get into the account for years. We worked with them to develop strategies that enticed prospective customers to say, "Tell me more"—and ultimately invite them in. The result? Eighty-seven percent of the reps achieved their goal within two months. (*Share a Success Story*)

Engage

So tell me—how is your company doing with new customer acquisition? Is it more challenging this year than last? (*Engage Your Prospect*)

That's what you need to say to pass the "Tell Me More" test. This message emphasizes the issue, shows success through real-life customer achievements, and then keeps the conversation going.

You need to practice and prepare as if everything depends on it—because it does. Get it right and you gain access. Slip back into sales talk and you'll find yourself in the dreaded D-Zone.

14

iNvaluable:
Become Irresistible Right Away

Wouldn't it be nice if it took just one call to get your foot in the door? Unfortunately, we all know better than that. Frazzled people are hard to reach. To get some of their precious time, we must spread multiple contacts out over time. And we need to ensure that what we do in those connections makes a difference.

So far we've focused on strategies you can use to increase alignment, focus on priorities, and simplify your message. Just by paying attention to these SNAP Factors, you're already setting yourself apart from 90 percent of all sellers. But don't rest on your laurels just yet. You still need to get the appointment.

Some sales experts tell you it's impossible to provide real value until you're actually working with a customer. I disagree. Before you connect, there are innumerable things you can do to demonstrate your commitment to their success, showcase your expertise, and make you worth meeting.

But be advised, by practicing these strategies you'll fundamentally alter your relationship with prospective customers. Instead of trying to overcome objections, you'll quickly find yourself immersed in substantive discussions regarding their key business challenges. Rather than being dismissed as another self-serving salesperson or a lightweight, you'll be welcomed into meetings to share information, ideas, and insights.

This is what sellers dream of happening. Here are some more things you can do to turn this dream into a reality.

Be the Resource Center

When you initially go after an account, plan on approximately ten touches (via phone, e-mail, and direct mail) spread out over four to six weeks. This condensed time frame is a real switch from the past.

You don't have to worry anymore about being a pest! With crazy-busy customers, your message doesn't even make it into their short-term memory. That's also why you need to condense your account entry campaign. Good messaging combined with educational resources makes you memorable and sets the stage for a valuable discussion.

While it's tempting to follow up with a "just checking in" message, that's the worst thing you can do. Every single communication needs to provide value. Since many of your connections will be via e-mail, this gives you an opportunity to link to quality content or attach it to your message.

Smart companies will create their own educational materials or events that span the issues, questions, and concerns of their customers at all phases of their decision-making process. Smart sellers will constantly be on the lookout for good information they can use, too. While it's helpful to have your company name on this information, it's not essential.

According to Ardath Albee, author of *eMarketing Strategies for the Complex Sale*, "Content designed for your prospects should present business value, help build a business case, educate about problems, invite interaction across the buying cycle, share expertise and reduce the perception of risk."

Think about articles, white papers, e-books, case studies, tips booklets, videos, seminars, podcasts, or Webinars with titles such as:

- How to Increase . . .
- 5 Strategies to . . .
- New Trends Impacting . . .
- How a Similar Firm Achieved . . .
- 7 Key Considerations in Selecting . . .
- What the New Legislation Means for . . .
- How to Overcome . . .

Get the picture? In your e-mails, you can send links, attachments, and invites to your prospects. This isn't a bunch of marketing mumbo jumbo. It's valuable content that will help them do their job better.

You can easily drop your prospect an e-mail like this one:

> As I mentioned last week, I know that one of your key strategic initiatives this year is new client acquisition.
>
> That's why I thought you'd be interested in this article published by CSO Insights. It highlights their recent

findings from their Lead-Generation Optimization Study.
[provide link]

> Also, I have some ideas about how to speed up your sales
> cycle and get more new clients in your pipeline before
> year-end. Let's set up a time to talk.

See how easy it is. Such an e-mail is businesslike, informative, and helpful. Just what customers want—and so much better than "just checking in to see if you've decided to do anything yet."

Account executive Nina Millhouse is a master of these keep-in-touch strategies. Here's an e-mail she recently sent to a hospital she was trying to get into.

> One of the most common methods of prescription fraud
> occurs when forms are stolen from busy exam rooms. I
> know your hospital is moving as fast as you can into
> ePrescribing, but it takes time. Until it's implemented,
> you need to keep your guard up.

> I realize it's short notice, but I have a recognized guru
> on prescription fraud in town next Tuesday. Would it be
> possible for us to gather the stakeholders of the
> ePrescribing initiative for a meeting?

> If you'd like to learn more, let me know. We can get
> something on the calendar.

Most sellers feel much better about this approach. It makes them feel valuable and vital, as opposed to being a desperate seller pathetically checking in one more time. And the reason they feel important is because they are.

Upgrade Your Digital Image

While we now have online access to all sorts of information about our prospects, the reverse is also true. Customers can check you out in detail prior to agreeing to meet. In a best-case scenario, your company Web site would be a resource hub, filled with invaluable content like we've just described. But if you can't control that, it doesn't mean all hope is lost.

You have 100 percent control of your personal online brand and should exercise it judiciously. The first place you need to start is with LinkedIn. Yes, we're back there again, but that's where your prospects will go first.

Your LinkedIn profile needs to be well written, with a special emphasis on your current position. Share your responsibilities, mention your achievements, and highlight your expertise. Make sure to avoid any self-promoting puffery, because that cheapens you. Be transparent and genuine. Look at the profile from your prospect's perspective: When they read it, will they want to do business with you?

To maximize your LinkedIn profile, use these strategies that savvy sellers have already discovered:

Get and give endorsements. Ask your current customers to post endorsements of you. They'll be glad to if you've done a good job for them. Ask your colleagues, boss, and coworkers, too. Be generous in return. When prospects check you out, they'll be impressed.

Join a variety of groups. Find ones that your prospects would be interested in. Ask questions and offer advice, but never sell. This subtle way of demonstrating expertise attracts people to you.

Update your status frequently. Once you've connected with your prospects, all your status updates show up on their home page. This is a great way to stay in front of them. Show them you're busy, refer them to good info sources, talk about trends, and share your wins.

"Answers"

Answer LinkedIn questions. There's a special section of Linked In called Answers, where people can post questions on a variety of business topics. Again, think like your prospect and figure out in what Linked In categories they'd be asking questions. Answer the ones that enable you to showcase your expertise. You might also want to pose your own questions to gain more insights into how your prospects think.

Post a SlideShare presentation. Create high-quality PowerPoint presentations to share relevant expertise on business issues, objectives, challenges, and trends. This gives your prospects a taste of what you're like to work with.

Here's what Keith Sheardown, general manager, Technology Solutions, at Bombardier Transportation, has to say about using this approach:

Recently I sent out invites to seven people in an account I'd targeted and they all accepted. When my primary customer replied, he mentioned the work we'd done with another transit agency. (I'd posted info about how our technology had reduced their inventory by 6 percent.)

We've already had three discussions now and are brainstorming what he can do. He's relying on me as an expert, even though he hasn't seen anything from me on what I actually sell. Now he wants me to come to his agency and spend two days reviewing their business, strategies, and potential next steps.

How did this happen? My LinkedIn profile speaks of my team, our current projects and what we've done to help transit agencies. I'm constantly revising it with the latest ROI.

Your LinkedIn profile is a great place to showcase yourself *and* your products or services. But you need to make sure that it always delivers value. Once you've done that, make sure to include a link to your profile in your signature file at the end of your e-mails. After all, it's a sales tool that shows people how you personally can make a difference.

Strategies of the Movers and Shakers

Because you'll inevitably hold multiple jobs in your career, you need to think about your personal brand. Sure, it will evolve over time. But what is it that you stand for today? How can you demonstrate this to prospective customers?

"Developing your brand makes you a more valuable asset," says Dan Schawbel, author of *Me 2.0: Build a Powerful Brand to Achieve Career Success*. "The successful brand YOU marketing model has the proper mix of confidence, passion, likeability, determination and focus."

LinkedIn is certainly a starting place. But if you really want to stand out from the crowd, start your own blog. Do it even if you don't have a ton of experience. If you have a blog, you should post once or twice per week on a topic that's relevant to your prospective customers.

More than anything else, blogs build credibility. Prospects

can get a good sense of who you are, how you think, and the potential value you can provide. Plus, if you do well, people will find you online and reach out to establish a connection.

Here are just a few ideas to get you started:

- If you read an interesting article, write a paragraph sharing your perspectives and then provide a link to it.
- If you hear a good speaker at a conference, record a five-minute interview with this person and post it on your blog.
- If you have a customer who's getting great results, record a video testimonial from this person detailing their initial status quo, the business issues they've faced, and the results they've achieved so far.
- If you're launching a new product, write about the business problems it addresses or its unique capabilities.
- If you see a relevant video on YouTube, explain why you think it's pertinent and link to it.

If you're in the CRM field, focus on Sales 2.0–related topics. If you sell promotional products, focus on how companies use them to achieve their objectives. If you work for a printing company, focus on trends in the printing industry.

When you write a blog, you'll uncover opportunities you could never have known about any other way. People will find you online. Your content will demonstrate your expertise. Then they'll contact you—already predisposed to work with you and feeling like they know you.

Building and maintaining your digital presence takes time. But the payback can be huge, especially when you keep this in mind—always provide value. When you do, you become an invaluable asset to a prospect, even before they become a customer.

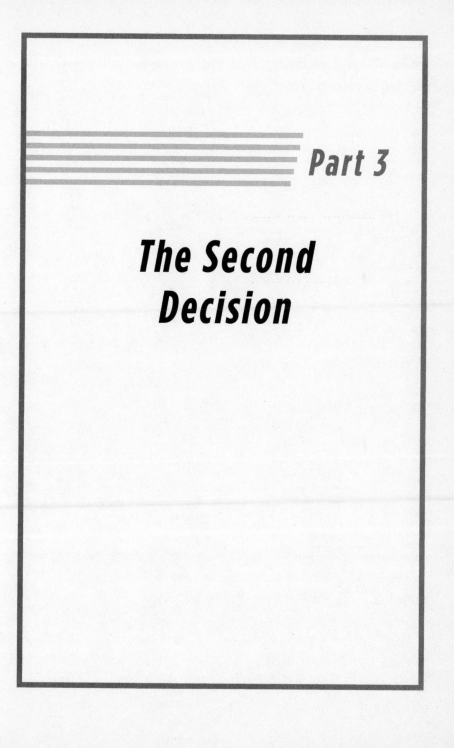

Part 3

The Second Decision

15

Second Decision Overview

Customer's Perspective

Now that you've piqued your prospects' curiosity enough, they're willing to set up a meeting with you. But getting them to accept the change you're offering is a whole different story, and depending on what you sell, it may take months. Here's what these frazzled customers are thinking while they're in this phase:

- I'm interested in learning more; you're speaking my language.
- If I like what I hear, I'm willing to investigate it to see if it's a good decision for us.
- That could be a ton of work, though, and I'm not sure I have the time.
- Even if the ROI (return on investment) is solid, success is still not guaranteed.
- Getting everyone's buy-in is a thankless undertaking.

Competition

These are your two primary competitors:

Status quo. Newton's Law of Inertia applies here: A body at rest tends to stay at rest. This is true of your customers, even if their current situation is less than perfect. It's their default setting. They're used to it and, if at all possible, would prefer to keep it that way. Any change is disruptive.

Mindshare. Your customer will constantly be pulled in other directions by everything else they're expected to do. New priorities will emerge, further adding to their workloads.

Risk and Fears

Your prospects fear they will be wasting time to determine if it makes good business sense to change and if it's even doable given all their constraints and challenges. Plus, they're afraid of sticking their necks out and possibly making a career-inhibiting decision.

What They Hate

- Sellers who come in with their "pitch" after promising a business-oriented conversation.
- Not having enough time to really think about their direction, and feeling like they're in a totally reactive, firefighting mode when they'd much prefer to be strategic.
- Having to deal with the slow process of getting all the stakeholders engaged and in agreement regarding the best way to move ahead.
- Sellers who await their direction or who just keep "checking in."

Seller's Role

People who suffer from Frazzled Customer Syndrome have high expectations from sellers whom they let into their world. In order to keep them engaged and move them to a point where it's imperative to move away from the status quo, it's important to:

- Go for conceptual buy-in as the critical first step.
- Ensure rock-solid alignment with their business goals and objectives.
- Provide leadership and guidance to help their decision making.

- Provoke their thinking and open them up to new possibilities.
- Scope out the potential value of making a change.
- Engage multiple people in the decision-making process early.
- Uncover any or all obstacles to their making a change.
- Continue offering valuable ideas, insights, and information.
- Make it easy for your prospects to do business with you.

Big Challenge

Inertia. The hardest part of this phase of the decision-making process is keeping it moving. The bigger, costlier, or riskier a decision is, the more likely your frazzled customer is to stay with the status quo. If the change initiative involves lots of extra work, the more likely it is to get delayed and, ultimately, derailed.

Mission Accomplished

You've accomplished your mission when your prospect says, "We have to change. The status quo is no longer acceptable. We'll never be able to reach our objectives if we continue with it. We need to make the investment soon. It's time to evaluate our options."

SNAP Considerations

Here's how the four SNAP Factors impact your prospects' second decision:

Simple: Being able to deliver a sizable impact to your prospects' organization isn't enough. The complexity of any change initiative can grind a buying decision to a screeching halt. The easier you can make it, the better your chances of success.

iNvaluable: By provoking your prospects' thinking, showing them better ways to do things, and guiding them through the complexities of making a decision, you'll be seen as a valuable asset—and part of the team. If they decide to move ahead, you will be in the driver's seat.

Aligned: If what you're talking about isn't relevant to their business objectives, they won't waste their time. However, crazy-busy people are always interested in ideas, insights, and information that can help them achieve their business objectives. Their focus is also on the size and scope of your offering's impact. Bigger is better.

Priority: Keeping the change initiative a high priority requires a rigorous commitment to rooting out all possible issues that could bog down the decision-making process.

Final Caveat

Working with a prospect at this stage of their decision-making process is *all about change*. Your product or service is virtually irrelevant. The only thing that matters is whether your offering will help them achieve their objectives.

Conceptual buy-in comes as a result of bringing your prospects ideas that (1) unearth unidentified problems that hurt their business; (2) provide a solution to an unsolvable problem; or (3) show them how to capitalize on an unseen opportunity.

You need to be the change agent that spearheads the initiative and keeps it moving. Sellers who get really good at the strategies in this section go into the third decision as part of the team. In many cases, crazy-busy prospects decide to do business with them without all the rigamarole of presentations, RFPs, or detailed proposals. They say, "Let's get going."

That's why it's imperative for your long-term sales success to really focus on the strategies in the upcoming chapters. In them, I try to provoke your thinking, give you ideas on how you can speed things up, validate business value, simplify the decision-making process, become part of the decision-making team, and establish yourself as an invaluable resource.

16

Getting Off to a Good Start

Kudos! You're now in a position that many sellers strive for but few achieve. Just think of all those deleted e-mails, unreturned phone calls, and tossed letters—the debris of sellers who weren't willing to pay the "price of admission." Your up-front research combined with your careful crafting of pertinent and timely messages made the difference.

You've earned the right to meet with potential customers. The opportunity to make a significant impact on their business or their lives looms before you. There's also the potential for significant financial gain on your part. But that'll happen only if you "do good" by your customers.

As you enter the second decision, the only thing you can absolutely be sure of is that you've piqued someone's interest. Perhaps your value proposition appealed to them or they're struggling with issues you identified. Maybe they're interested in the ideas you suggested. That's enough to get started.

Ooh, the Possibilities!

There's nothing I like better than engaging prospects when they're not thinking of making any changes. This may seem counterintuitive if you've spent your career chasing prospects already in the buying mode—the "low-hanging fruit," as I call them. However, here are a few things to consider before you go after these supposedly "easy" opportunities:

The incumbent is sleeping. Since dislodging the status quo is your biggest challenge, you want to slip in under the existing provider's radar screen. By bringing in fresh perspectives that help prospects better achieve their objectives, you gain a foothold in an otherwise impenetrable account. The incumbent's failure to do so creates a credibility gap for them and opens the door for you.

Your competitors aren't around. If you do things right, you'll prove your capabilities, demonstrate your expertise, and establish a strong relationship long before any competitors enter the scene. They'll be playing catch-up from the start and, in most cases, will find it extremely difficult to close the gap.

You set the playing field. By bringing new ideas, insights, and information to the decision maker, you'll help determine the criteria against which future "go-ahead" decisions will be judged. This gives you a chance to best position the strengths of your product, service, or solution.

Sales cycles get condensed. When you leverage your expertise to help customers sort through everything that has to be considered to make a change, their decision-making process goes faster.

Customers often love you. Okay, I don't mean literally. But if you've ever had someone show you a better way, then made it simple to implement it, you know what I mean. That's how I feel when I visit the Apple Genius Bar, where tech gurus show me how to solve seemingly insoluble problems on my computer.

As you can see, there are many good reasons to get engaged with a prospective customer earlier rather than later.

What If There's No Money in the Budget?

Budget schmudget! I know you've been told that it's important to work with people who already have funds allocated for your offering. I know you've been chastised for not asking that question up front. And I also know you need business now—not next year, when budgets are reshuffled.

But that's shortsighted thinking. Here's what you don't realize: While the total amount in the budget may remain consistent, how it's allocated can change overnight. For example, when I sold copiers for Xerox, if a machine broke down, companies found a way to pay for it—even though it wasn't in their budget. Many chose to finance their new acquisition so the payments would have minimal impact on their operations.

Later on, when I sold for a technology company, after I

showed my prospects the increased productivity and significant savings they could realize by making a change, they found money in their budget for that change. Of course, some other projects were defunded.

When I sold my services as a product launch consultant, no one ever had money in their budget; they didn't even know people like me existed. However, when they saw the impact I could have on sales, they reallocated their budget or asked for more funding.

Never let the lack of money in the budget stop you. Every single day, in every single company, people change their priorities about how to spend their money. When the economy is struggling—as it is while I write this—CFOs are rethinking their budgets every ninety days to ensure they're most aligned with market conditions.

Don't wait for customers who are ready to buy. Be a sales initiator and learn how to create opportunities out of thin air.

If you bring prospects an idea that makes good business sense, they'll consider it. If the idea is aligned with their business objectives, strategic imperatives, or current priorities, it'll be evaluated. If they like what they see, money will be found.

That's the basis on which I've always operated. It's how I've trained people for years. And it works far better than chasing the low-hanging fruit that a gazillion competitors are fighting over.

The Tyranny of the Status Quo

This doesn't mean everything will magically fall into place. Depending on what you sell, along with its complexity, associated risk, costs to acquire, and numerous other factors, your prospect's decision-making process may extend for many months.

In her groundbreaking book *Dirty Little Secrets*, sales expert Sharon Drew Morgen points out that most sales training and salespeople totally ignore "the majority of the confusing, risky and hidden change issues buyers need to address behind-the-scenes before they can responsibly bring in a new solution."

She's absolutely right. We can't ignore these things any longer, because they impact our ability to move ahead.

A few years back, I was doing a project for a large manufacturing company. We were tackling a major change initiative with how the company launched new products. I remember telling the executive I was working with, "I feel like I'm a small puff of wind that's trying to get an ocean liner to change direction. Every time I stop blowing, even for only one second, it goes back to its original course."

Your customers' status quo is the original course. Everything in their ecosystem is set up to maintain their current way of doing things—even if it's not the best way to get the work done. They may know it, or they may be blissfully ignorant that their ways are outdated or underperforming.

It doesn't matter. The devil they know is easier to deal with than the devil they don't. They may have contracts that prohibit them from doing things differently, procedures that detail the exact processes to follow, and even entire departments or infrastructures that support their legacy systems or methodologies.

Not only that, you're walking into a customer's ecosystem that potentially has people who:

- Could lose their jobs if they brought in your solution.
- Worked with your company in the past and had a bad experience.

- Would rather do the work internally than use an external resource.
- Would feel bad ending a long-standing vendor relationship.
- Are involved in turf wars with others on the decision-making team.
- Have future plans to which you're not privy.
- Don't believe a change would work for them.

There are hundreds of valid reasons for keeping things the same. With frazzled customers, it can take even longer to bring about change, because the sheer number of distractions prevents them from focusing on your ideas, products, or services.

Change Is a Lot of Work

Recently I had a conversation with the CEO of a software company. He was having a major rant about his company's targeted customer: "VPs of Sales are the laziest people I've ever seen. We clearly have a product that significantly increases sales productivity, drives revenue growth, and improves margins. Yet they always have some excuses for not moving ahead."

He's right about the value of his offering. It does bring high value. He's dead wrong about VPs of Sales being lazy. They're under extreme pressure to deliver results; their job literally depends on it. While they'd love the benefits of change, they also think about the challenges of integrating with current systems, training non-tech-savvy sellers, the failures of previous CRM implementations, the cost of pulling sales reps out of the field, and the extra work needed to build the sales tools.

And if these Sales VPs have never made CRM decisions before, they also think about the extra time it would take to get up to speed on making a good decision, gaining the support of everyone involved (especially the naysayers), coordinating cross-functional decisions, justifying the value of the decision, and more.

Sometimes it just seems easier to stay with the status quo, which former U.S. president Ronald Reagan defined as "Latin for 'the mess that we're in.'"

But it doesn't have to be that way! You can lead your prospects through the second decision by leveraging the SNAP Factors.

Besides, when you can clearly articulate the value you bring them—and when you realize that it's your responsibility to address these status quo constraints, it won't take forever to persuade your prospects to change. Your guidance on how to make these important decisions will strengthen your own credibility and position you as an invaluable asset. Be glad that your competitors are clueless to the possibilities.

17

Mind Over Chatter

Your initial meeting is the most important one you'll ever have with your prospect. It's a gateway meeting, an opportunity for your prospective customer to determine if they'll keep the conversation going or send you into the dreaded D-Zone, where sellers are routinely dismissed because they lack the SNAP.

That's right. Those picky prospects are evaluating you from the moment your meeting convenes until it ends. All the while, they're asking themselves: How relevant is this to my business objectives? Is it a priority? How much effort will it take to change? Does this seller personally bring value?

Sophisticated, informed customers are far more selective than you might imagine. In fact, recent research by CSO Insights shows that 53 percent of sales organizations report that less than half of their first meetings resulted in a second meeting. Just four years ago only 43 percent of sales forces had such poor conversion results. According to managing partner Jim Dickie, this 25 percent increase represents an "alarming erosion in sales rep effectiveness."

What was the biggest difference between companies that did well versus those that struggled? Easy access to insights and knowledge about their prospects' company, marketplace, competitor, and even the decision makers.

In short, you must prepare for these initial meetings. Your buyers have higher expectations of you than ever before. Your natural charm or ability to schmooze might make you feel like you're establishing a good relationship, but it doesn't lead to a follow-up meeting. "Winging it" doesn't work. Until you understand this in your bones, you'll have a tough time in sales.

Homework Required

Now that we know preparation is essential, the question is: What do you need to study? To be most effective, here are some things you can do prior to your initial meeting:

- Review your prospects' Web site and annual report. Get a good sense of what their company (division) does, the challenges they face, the market trends impacting them, and their key strategic imperatives.
- Look at their press releases. Learn the most up-to-date information about what's happening in the organization.
- Listen to management presentations in the Investor Relations area of their Web site. In these, you can get current info about their biggest challenges and

strategic imperatives. Also attend any upcoming presentations.

- Identify other customers similar to this prospect. Think about how you've helped them, the results they've attained, and the challenges they faced.
- Subscribe to any newsletters the company might have. This will keep you in-the-know over a period of time.

Next, review your Buyer's Matrix. Make sure you're intimately familiar with each decision maker's position. If you've created a persona, you'll want to be prepared to do a mind meld.

Finally, start thinking about the best way to shape this information so that you can have the highest impact in your first meeting. You're going to need it, because your frazzled prospects will demand it!

Solving a Kronick Problem

No, I didn't spell *chronic* wrong. Years ago I had a prospect named Mr. Kronick, who was president of a metal recycling company. I was a trainee at Xerox, making cold calls in northeast Minneapolis, the one and only time I met Mr. Kronick. After telling the receptionist that I'd like to speak to the person who made copier decisions, she made a quick call to the boss. When he agreed to see me, she led me across a vast office filled with people busy doing order entry.

Mr. Kronick was a short man with few social graces. After a perfunctory handshake, he said, "You've got five minutes. Talk."

"But I can't possibly find out all about your needs in that time," I said, startled by his abruptness.

"Like I said, you've got five minutes. Talk!" he repeated. Then he pulled out a sand timer and set it on the desk. "When it's done, you're done."

I was appalled. I couldn't possibly do my job as a consultative seller if he was going to behave that way. The man was clearly not cooperating. "Mr. Kronick, five minutes isn't nearly enough to have a thorough understanding of your needs and make a recommendation," I stammered. "If you're busy right now I'd be glad to come back at a later time."

He didn't answer me. Instead, he just pointed at the timer. I started to panic. The next thing I knew, I was babbling something stupid about our full-range of copiers, our incredible like-for-like replacement policy, and how we took better care of our customers than the dealer network.

All the while, my eyes were watching the grains of sand drop. I couldn't talk fast enough. When they were all gone, Mr. Kronick stood up, extended his hand, and said, "Thanks for coming in today. I need to get back to work."

Mortified at his behavior, I stuffed all my brochures back into my briefcase. Then, taking great umbrage, I stormed out of his office and past his staff, yelling, "You are the rudest man I've ever met. I will never, ever let Xerox sell you a copier."

Xerox probably never got that chance! In fact, I pity the sales rep who followed me into that territory. I was a hard act to follow.

What's the message here? Mr. Kronick is just like today's crazy-busy customer. He expected me to "net it out." My job was to do that.

Not only was I totally unprepared, but I felt a sense of moral superiority because I was a consultative seller. Let me assure you, that combination will doom you to the D-Zone.

The Death of Consultative Selling

Don't get me wrong! I love being a consultative seller. But a few years ago I discovered that "being consultative" wasn't the best way to start an initial meeting. My prospects wanted more. Just like my friend Mr. Kronick, they wanted me to "net it out."

Initially I was horribly resistant; it just didn't feel right. I wanted to spend a few minutes warming up the relationship, engaging in pleasant chit-chat and building a relationship. And the last thing I wanted to do was to "assume"; it was drilled into me that to do so would make an "ASS-out-of-U-and-ME."

But when you're living in a world of Mr. Kronicks, that approach doesn't work anymore. Today you need to make assumptions. You need to assume that your current prospect has similar situations, issues, needs, and concerns as similar companies in their industry. You need to assume that the decision makers have similar objectives and goals. You need to assume that the marketplace trends are impacting them in a similar manner. Of course, there will be variations. You can get to that later. Right now, you first need to show your prospects that you're worth knowing.

These busy buyers don't want to answer your consultative questions right away, either. Imagine a seller starting a conversation this way:

> Thank you for meeting with me today. As I mentioned, we specialize in state-of-the-art services to help companies like yours with all your solution needs. Of course, I'd never assume to know your needs. Every business is different, so I have a few questions to ask you:

- How are you currently handling things?
- What's keeping you up at night?
- If you could wave a magic wand, what would you change?

Unfortunately, this seller would be immediately consigned to the D-Zone. They haven't established credibility or built the proper foundation for a conversation. Now contrast it to this approach:

> Glad to meet you. As I mentioned on the phone, I know how much the economy is impacting manufacturing firms like yours. That's why we've been focusing on companies in this market segment for the past six months.
>
> What we've found is that many of these manufacturers are paying way too much for their software licenses—especially since there have been so many organizational changes and downsizings.
>
> We've been able to trim their expenses by up to 22.7 percent in the first year. Let me give you a couple of examples so you can see if they ring true to you. Then we can talk about your situation in more detail.

You have to prove you're a viable player before customers open up to you. So the first thing you need to do is start assuming—even though you've been trained not to. At the start of new relationships, demonstrate your expertise up front. That's how you earn the right to be consultative and have those candid conversations.

Keeping Your Promise

Remember that tightly worded voice-mail or e-mail message you crafted to get your foot in the door? Refer back to that when you set up your initial meeting.

For instance, if you stated that you'd like to get together to talk about a specific business issue your prospects face, be prepared to do that. If you mentioned that you have some ideas on how to achieve an important business objective, focus on that at the start of your conversation. Or if you talked about the results your current customers are achieving from using your offering, expand on that.

That was the premise under which your prospects agreed to meet. Failure to start the meeting with this as your primary focus is a violation of their trust.

Unfortunately, that's exactly what more than 50 percent of sellers are doing, and that's why they're having such trouble. Somehow, there's a disconnect in their brain between what they said to get the meeting and what they do once they get there.

So what do these sellers do? They feel compelled to start out the meeting with an overview of their firm's history, provide a customer list, and then launch into a spiel about their products, services, or solution. They do this regardless of the type of meeting they've scheduled, whether it's a Webinar, phone conversation, or a face-to-face.

Whenever sellers I'm coaching do this, I say, "Why are you talking about that?" The answer I invariably hear is, "They need to know this about us."

No, they don't. Sellers have an overwhelming compulsion to relate this garbage. Perhaps the boss or marketing people told them to do it. But let me be clear here: Your prospects don't need to know this at the onset. The only thing they care about is if you bring value to their business. If not, you're a waste of time.

Speaking of waste: Keep your brochures at home. If you bring them with you, you will feel compelled to show them to your prospects. When you do, you invariably move into "pitch" mode, where you start to sell. That's also a violation of trust. You said you were there to talk about business issues and challenges. And there you are, yammering on about your unique capabilities, robust systems, or state-of-the-art methodologies? Broken promises aren't good.

Go into sales calls totally naked. (That's how many sellers feel if they leave their brochures at home!) It'll be awkward at first, but you'll get much better results. Otherwise, you'll be dismissed so graciously you won't even know the meeting is over. Instead of an opportunity, you've been sent to the D-Zone.

18

Meetings That SNAP, Crackle, and Pop

What do you consider the purpose of your initial meeting? Let me guess. You want to understand your prospects' needs better. You want to impress them with your outstanding products or services. And if everything goes well, you'd love for them to place their first order with you. Right?

Wrong, wrong, wrong! Your initial objective is to get them to understand what's possible if they work with you and your company. At the end of your meeting, short as it may be, your prospects should willingly allot time on their already overflowing calendar for whatever the next logical step turns out to be.

That's exactly what the top sellers do. They get even the most frazzled customers to say, "Let's get going. I'm interested."

Lighting That Initial Spark

What exactly does it take to light that spark of possibility? Years ago, when I coached a creative problem-solving team, I had a chance to compare how fourteen-year-old girls presented their ideas, and their peers' reaction to them during our practices.

My own daughter spent hours coming up with innumerable creative ideas, yet few were accepted. Her detailed presentation, personal attachment to the concept, plus its completeness weren't enough to engage her peers. Another girl offered her ideas tentatively, unsure if they were good enough. Unsurprisingly, the group usually passed on them. But a third girl nearly always had her half-baked ideas accepted. Here's what she said:

> You guys! I've been thinking. You know how we were talking about how we'd handle that challenge. Last night, I came up with this great idea. Here's what we can do . . . So what do you think? Cool, huh!

Her confident and passionate delivery stoked everyone's interest from the outset. Her description about what was possible kept them engaged. And in the end, she invited them to join her.

Rosamund and Benjamin Zander sum up this concept in their book, *The Art of Possibility.* "Enrolling is not about forcing, cajoling, tricking, bargaining, pressuring or guilt-tripping someone into doing things your way," they say. "Enrollment is the art and practice of generating a spark of possibility for others to share."

People who are "enrolled" want to get involved. They believe it's worth it, that a positive result—perhaps one they'd never even thought of before—is possible. There's a palpable excitement about learning more, advancing the cause, studying the problem, and engaging the troops.

The principles at the core of enrollment may seem like sales heresy to traditionalists, but they're really the foundation of all good selling.

Let go of the outcome. If you want something badly (such as a next meeting), people can smell it. They feel your need, your pandering, your push, or even your desperation. Stop focusing on the sale.

Focus on the possibilities. Paint the picture of the tangible outcomes so your prospects can see themselves as part of it. In order to do this well, you really need to understand your value proposition and the difference you can make for your customers.

It's not about your product or service. It's all about the difference it can make for them. Tie your idea into what's happening in their company. Make sure they know this is all about them achieving their results—not you getting a sale.

Extend the invitation. Invite them to figure out how you can work together, what you need to explore next, and who else needs to get involved.

Recently I approached a state agency with an idea for helping people who were struggling to find employment in a down economy. I'd just finished writing *Get Back to Work Faster*, a book that shows people how to find hidden job opportunities or create new ones. I was also offering a series of free Webinars on the topic. But I wanted to make a bigger impact—which is why I set up a meeting with the job services agency.

My challenge? They'd never done anything like what I was presenting. They had no money in their budget. And my solution to their problem would require multiple unconnected agencies to work together.

In the first meeting, I focused entirely on engagement. I started with a compelling story, shared my concept about the value it provided, raised the issues I knew about, and opened the meeting up for discussion: Sound interesting? What do you think? What do we need to do next?

As I write this, I don't know the final outcome. But I do know I have multiple people working with me at the state agency to see if we can turn our vision into reality.

When you learn how to enroll people, you transform their skepticism into anticipation. And they're willing to move ahead with you even if they don't have all the details or know exactly where you're going. You've engaged them in making things better—even if it ultimately involves something as mundane as purchasing a copier.

Here's your challenge. Take a look at your own initial meetings. Are you enrolling prospects in the possibilities? Are they moving ahead with you, excited about what they can potentially accomplish? What, if anything, do you need to change to light that initial spark?

You've Got Five Minutes—Talk!

Remember Mr. Kronick from chapter 17? Have you thought about what you'd do if your prospects gave you only five minutes? Today's frazzled customers prefer these short initial meetings, and you need to get through them if you want their dedicated time and attention. If you're not prepared, it's time to get your act together.

You should consider using these mini-meetings as a foot-in-the-door strategy. The less time you ask for, the more likely your request will be granted. You can have these meetings in person, schedule a conference call, or request an online meeting.

The key to your success is highly correlated to how well you can "net it out"—in other words, how well you get to the point, show them the value they'll get and why they should pay attention. And if you remember from the first decision, the less time you have with someone, the more time you need to invest ensuring that you deliver the right message. Still, most sellers think a five-minute meeting is no big deal. They're overconfident in their verbal skills, and consider a five- or fifteen-minute conversation a no-brainer.

Let me be blunt. Unless you prep for that meeting, you will blow it. You may have a great conversation. You may think you're building a relationship. But you're not. You're missing the opportunity to enroll this person in what's possible. Now. With your company.

What goes into your mini-meeting? It's time to do a SNAP Check again. Remember, your success is contingent on your being in the Go Zone with each SNAP Factor.

Simple	Complex
▲	

Invaluable	Ordinary
▲	

Aligned	Irrelevant
▲	

Priority	Nicety
▲	
GO Zone	D-Zone

Look at what you've prepared from your prospect's perspective. Do the mind meld. Be ruthless with what you decide to say, the questions you choose to ask, or the slides you elect to show.

If anything is irrelevant or nonessential, chuck it. You can talk about it later.

Case in Point

Technology sales rep Lynn Hidy wanted to increase her sales to a major agribusiness firm. She did her homework and had a good understanding of what was going on in the company. But her numerous attempts to connect with the divisional IT director had failed. So she proposed a mini-meeting by sending the woman a stopwatch with the following note:

> I know you're busy. I only need three minutes of your time to ask you two questions. Then you can determine if it's even worth it to continue our conversation. To see if I keep my first commitment, I've included a stopwatch so you can time me.

Shortly after, the IT director's assistant called to set up a three-minute call. After a very brief introduction highlighting her research and value proposition, Lynn asked her first question:

> What would your business be like if all your vendors were looking for creative ways to drive your IT projects in on time and under budget?

Initially, the IT director was stumped; she couldn't give her automatic reaction. Then she started to open up about what her vision of that could look like. When they approached the three-minute mark, Lynn said:

I want to keep my first commitment to you about time. We're approaching the end now. Would it make sense to keep talking to see if I can be the first vendor to work with you on that?

What shocked Lynn was the response—the IT director of a billion-dollar company asked her if she had time to continue the conversation. The end result? According to Lynn, "A very nice contract that just keeps getting better."

You don't have to have a Kronick problem like I did. With some planning, you can use mini-meetings as a way to establish your credibility and demonstrate your commitment to helping your customers achieve their high-priority business objectives.

Setting the Agenda

Great sales meetings don't just miraculously happen. They're the result of thinking and strategizing about what it takes to get to a successful outcome. Since busy decision makers want to ensure that their time is well spent, one of the best things you can do is to prepare an agenda for the meeting. If you're getting together with someone for the first time, e-mail a copy of it to the person you're meeting, with a short accompanying note like this one:

I look forward to getting together on Tuesday to talk about how we can reduce time to revenue on new product introductions. In preparation for the meeting, I've attached an agenda. If I've missed anything, let me know, since I want to make sure you get the maximum value from our time together.

Notice the focus? It's all about what your prospects get out of the meeting. Sending an agenda will always be perceived positively. It doesn't have to be perfect to get a good reaction. Your prospects will see you as a class act who willingly invests time up front to ensure the meeting is worth their while.

Well-planned meetings typically start with a short overview that positions the meeting and reiterates your business purpose for being there. You also need to spend a few minutes painting a picture of what's possible and enrolling your prospects into this idea. Then, you'll move to a conversation about their current situation, goals, and objectives—a discussion guided by you.

That's where the agenda comes in. I'll never forget the first time I met with Todd Johnson, a certified financial planner my husband and I use for our personal finances. After a few moments of setting the stage, he pulled out an agenda and reviewed it with us. Impressed with his professionalism, I relaxed into the meeting.

His agenda looked like this, but included numerous sub-bulleted items to denote specific topics.

JOHN AND JANE SMITH
FINANCIAL REVIEW
- Review questions/concerns
- Client update
- Economic update
- Account review
- Goal discussion

- Review fundamentals
- Next meeting date

Todd's clients really value this approach. In fact, his company regularly surveys its clients, and they consistently give him a 98 percent satisfaction rating! I asked him to share the thinking that went into creating his agenda. Here's what he said:

> I always start with what's on my client's mind. It doesn't do any good to plunge into my objectives. Next, I get an update on any changes. This helps me know them on a deeper level and builds trust. After that, I do an economic update. Because of the turmoil in the economy, many clients want to hear my take on this.
>
> After that, we talk about their account performance, allocations, and changes. We follow that with a goal discussion to allow my client to define what they want from their assets. Plus it helps me to properly design their portfolio. I also review important fundamentals. And finally, I set up the next meeting. I always want my client's expectation set as to when we'll get together next.

As a result of this preliminary planning, Todd aligns with client needs, keeps financial planning a priority, becomes an invaluable resource, and makes a complex subject simple. Is it any wonder that his clients value him?

Here's what you need to realize: it's the time spent planning the agenda that increases your success rate—not the document itself. The physical product is a visible sign to your prospects that you've invested time preparing for the meeting with them.

Remember, your agenda is simply a guide, not a commit-ment to a rigid schedule. You or your prospect may want to take the meeting in another direction. Plus, if you don't get it all done in one sitting, you now have a very good reason for a follow-up conversation.

But all this is a moot point if you don't have a solid business case for working with your prospect's company—which is what we'll talk about next.

19

Aligned: Assessing Business Value

The easiest way to win more sales is to have a strong business case. That's why we've spent so much time focusing on your value propositions. Being able to clearly articulate the business value of your offering is critical for getting your foot in the door. But it's really just a start.

Your role during the second decision is to move your crazy-busy prospects off their sense of complacency with their current situation. You need to explore the potential effect your product, service, or solution can have on their organization. If it's aligned with their business objectives and priorities—and if they feel it's "do-able"—they'll likely commit to making a change.

Basically, frazzled prospects want to fix important problems or boost results with the least disruption. Sometimes they are aware that there are issues with the status quo, but they don't fully understand the consequences of doing nothing. At other times they have no idea there's a better way to do things, since they've lived with these aggravations for so long. They're totally oblivious to the costly work-arounds that have evolved over the years. It's just "how we do things here."

Then there are the prospects who are expected to achieve a challenging objective. While they're looking to boost results, they're still hoping to do it with what's in place right now.

A major key to your success lies in your ability to co-develop a strong business case with your prospects so that they'll willingly go to bat for you with their management team.

Questions Are the Answer

We've already talked about how to light that initial spark by sharing strong value propositions and enrolling your prospect into "what's possible." If you've targeted the right organizations and done your homework, then it's highly likely you're spot-on.

But even so, you need verification that your offering has value for them, *and* your prospects need to find this out for themselves. From the outside, there's only so much you can know. You still need to find out the particulars of their status quo, their business objectives or strategic imperatives, their priorities, and the impact you could have on their company.

In short, you're lacking what it takes to build a strong case for their using your product or service. You don't even know if it's a decent fit.

That's why you must ask questions to assess the business value of your offering. When sellers learn to ask good questions, their prospects evaluate them as more caring and concerned, and more knowledgeable about the prospects' jobs, market, and products.

Your ability to ask good questions cannot be left to chance. It's imperative to determine what you'll ask prior to meeting with prospective customers. Plan, plan, plan. I can't say this enough.

There's a good reason for it, too. Research shows that your brain is not capable of processing two distinctly different activities simultaneously. This means that when your prospect is talking, you can either listen or figure out what to say next. You can't do both.

If you're like most people, you try to jump back and forth between the two. Unfortunately, in doing this, you miss half of what your prospect is saying—which could include information relevant to your business case. Or your questions are superficial and shallow, thus preventing you from maximizing your precious time with your prospect.

Really good questions are often the key to significant changes in an organization. They have the power to:

- Channel your prospect's attention on what matters;
- Generate curiosity and stimulate interest in what's possible;
- Provoke reflection, insights and thought;
- Surface hidden assumptions; and
- Generate forward momentum.

Yet most sellers invest minimal time in thinking about what they're going to ask or how to frame and sequence questions for maximal impact.

Not Doyle Slayton, founder of SalesBlogCast.com. When he first connects with clients, he tells them, "The majority of my clients are coming from Competitor A and Competitor B, primarily because I've found big problems in the way they're billing small business owners. Some have saved over 50 percent on what they were previously paying."

But when he gets to the meeting, Doyle doesn't just focus on the financial savings. He knows that his odds of winning the business skyrocket when prospects discover they can get significantly more value from their investment—even after cutting their spending. As such, he's designed a series of questions to explore the issues and bottlenecks that can be eliminated by his service, and their financial ramifications. It's all planned from the get-go. He knows where he's going, yet he's still flexible enough to make changes based on what happens during the meeting.

Good planning makes this possible. You don't have a lot of time with crazy-busy buyers, so it's imperative that you use it wisely.

Juicy Conversations About Business Value

Justyn Howard, a highly successful enterprise account manager and author of *Sell Smarter*, says, "You're defined by the questions you ask. The quickest way to set yourself apart from your competition and add value to the process is through intelligent questions. People who ask the most thought-provoking questions win the hearts of decision makers every time." Amen.

How do you create these questions? By now you've laid the foundation for your juicy conversation and have completed a Buyer's Matrix on your primary decision makers. What's in that matrix becomes the foundation for creating questions that elicit business value.

Here's how it works. My targeted decision maker is the VP of Sales. If you look at the sample Buyer's Matrix from chapter 5, you'll see that this person's number one priority is revenue attainment—hitting the numbers. Lead generation and shortening the sales cycle are also key strategic initiatives. There are other things that are important, but these are areas I can affect.

Here are some of the questions you could ask if you were calling on this person, and my thinking behind them:

Can you give me an overview of your sales process?
This helps you get a lay of the land. It's also nonthreatening, and therefore a good discussion opener.

What impact is the economy having on your sales results this year? Will you be able to meet your numbers?
To get you focused on priority issues and demonstrate expertise, find out how timely trends or trigger events are impacting their business.

What are your people struggling with the most right now? What else?
This helps you determine the biggest issues and assess the business consequences of them.

What initiatives have you already implemented to help your salespeople with these issues? Why did you choose these initiatives?
Prospects have likely taken some steps to address the issues they're facing. You need to know what they've already done.

How satisfied are you with the results you're getting? Where do you still have gaps?

People typically use their own company resources before they look for outside help. You want to find out how well their homegrown solutions have worked.

You've mentioned a number of challenges. What are your priorities?

To ensure maximum alignment, it's essential to know what's most important from your prospect's perspective.

How are you leveraging Sales 2.0 technologies to increase sales force productivity?

If something impacts your ability to be successful, ask about it. Plus, if you discover they have little knowledge in an area, it shows you where you can bring value.

Notice how the questions are focused on the key business issues that my frazzled VP of Sales faces. That's what makes for a juicy conversation. The questions are of high interest to your prospects because they're about their life—not your product or service.

Use your Buyer's Matrix as a guide to develop relevant questions. Also, pay attention to how you ask the questions. Your goal is to get thoughtful answers that will help both you and your prospect determine if you can, in fact, provide business value.

Bring your preplanned questions to the meeting. When you take out your notebook, have your questions right there in front of you at all times. People *respect* this. Plus, it's what the very best sellers do. They're prepared to focus 100 percent of their time on the conversation—not in thinking about what to ask next.

Finding Bigger and Better Business Value

Recently I trained the sales force of a company that had just started selling document management solutions, a technology that scans, organizes, and processes paper documents. Their initial ROI analysis focused on the dollars that companies could save because they'd buy less paper, need fewer file cabinets, and would therefore require less office space.

When I saw the savings, I wasn't impressed. I couldn't see decision makers changing for these meager results. It would simply be too much work.

These salespeople were missing the bigger value they could offer: the impact on the cash conversion cycle and enhanced productivity. By switching to paperless processes, some of their customers were able to handle a 60 percent increase in workload with the same staff. Others cut their sales order processing time, bringing more money into the organization faster. CFOs who'd never been interested in this technology suddenly started drooling over the business impact.

How did the sellers miss all this? Because they came from the copier world, where they'd never considered those factors when building their business case.

Their situation is not unusual. Due to lack of experience, many sellers really don't know the business value of what they're solving. What follows are several strategies you can use to expand your knowledge and build a bigger, better business case.

Explore the Ripple Effect.

The Ripple Effect is based on the premise that problems aren't isolated events. Anytime something goes wrong, it has an impact on other things. One problem begets another.

To find all sorts of hidden ramifications in the problems that occur, be on high alert for these words:

difficulty   dissatisfaction   bottleneck   challenges   issues

frustration   aggravation   headache   trouble   concerns

Once you hear these indicator words, ask questions that explore the problems created by these problems. Look for the problems' business impact, the effect or ramifications they're having on other areas. Not only is this information helpful to you in building a business case for change, because you understand the Ripple Effect on their organization, it also enhances your credibility with prospects. You clearly know your stuff!

Look for the White Space.

Over the years, I've found tremendous opportunities emerging from the white space. What do I mean by this? If what you sell can impact multiple departments or divisions, look for what's not getting done or is being done haphazardly. If what you sell impacts a customer process (e.g., order processing or automobile assembly), explore what's happening upstream or downstream to find areas where you can add business value. This white space is an area that's between other areas where no one person is responsible. It's between groups. It's where people aren't paying attention, but where problems can arise and fester for years.

In my consulting business, the white space was the chasm between Sales and Marketing, especially when new products were launched. There were so many things that fell through the cracks that actually prevented companies from boosting their results the way they wanted.

Focus on the Future.

Your crazy-busy buyers are barreling full speed ahead toward achieving their ever-increasing objectives. Yet because they're too busy fighting fires, they've often given minimal thought to ensuring they have the optimal environment for achieving their goals.

Ask about their short- and long-term goals. What are they? What are the critical success factors for achieving them? Where are the potential vulnerabilities? Use this discussion to raise issues that you've seen other companies run into, and then explore their situation relevant to these challenges.

Being curious is good. In fact, when you pose these questions, you actually help crazy-busy buyers. And don't worry about being perceived as nosy. Your prospects expect you to raise these issues. That's what makes for a juicy conversation.

Pulling Together the Case for Change

Before an organization commits to change, it must have a valid business reason for moving ahead. The size, scope, and risk of what's being proposed often determine how detailed an analysis needs to be. They also impact how many people need to be involved in data gathering and decision making.

What's most important about the business case is that your customers believe it accurately represents the value that their company will realize if they embrace change. They need to be able to stand in front of a group three months from now and justify that they made a good decision.

Typically, decision makers want you to show:

Payback: the time it takes for the company to recover its investment costs and generate profits;

Return on Investment (ROI): the value expected to be gained by making a purchase; and

Total Cost of Ownership (TCO): the direct and indirect costs of using a product, service, or solution.

Sometimes you just need a rough estimate to get the ball rolling. But if your prospects need a detailed analysis, make sure you help them with it. Remember, they don't decide these things often and can overlook important elements.

Also, not everyone has to go through these financial gyrations to make change happen. People who sell ideas or their professional expertise may never create an official ROI document. When their prospects hear about new options or fresh approaches, they get excited and say, "Yes! I want to be a part of this. We need to do this." (That's where the art of enrollment comes in.)

While they may never have to come up with hard numbers, these prospects can confidently state to their bosses that "we had to do something different" or "it's the way the market is going, so we needed to do it, too." Both the customer and the seller are in alignment regarding what it will take to realize the organization's goals. They're buying "what's possible" and willing to move ahead on that basis alone.

Sales-Busting Mistakes

If you stay focused on how much benefit a prospective customer could gain from working with your company, you'll stay in the Go Zone. However, there are several egregious mistakes you can make that can send you spiraling into the D-Zone at the blink of an eye.

The Curse of Knowledge

Sometimes your own smarts get in your way. You assume that the person you're talking to has the same depth of understanding. When that happens, you fail to explore issues with your prospects because it's so blatantly obvious to you what's happening and what the consequences are.

Now is a time when you must never assume. Your questions educate your prospect (which builds your credibility) and help you collaborate in building the business case.

The Itch to Pitch

Unfortunately for most sellers, their itch to pitch is unleashed when they start hearing about their prospect's issues and challenges. Before you know it, they're leaning forward in their chair and talking excitedly about their offering or capabilities.

This is a setup for disaster. Sellers who do this are violating the rules of engagement. Remember, if you're selling to any organization, they're not going to make the decision on the spot. You'll need at least one or two—if not many—meetings before they'll be ready to make a decision. So when the itch to pitch overcomes you, fight it.

Now that you've convinced your prospects that you are aligned with their goals, you must demonstrate that moving ahead is doable. That's what we'll tackle next.

20

iNvaluable: Become the Expert
They Can't Live Without

Recently I met with executives from two very different businesses. One company sold products that cost a couple of thousand dollars; the other sold services costing hundreds of thousands annually. Yet both had one thing in common: Even though they felt their offering was significantly different from that of their competitors, their prospects didn't.

You've probably experienced the same thing. In today's market, it's virtually impossible to maintain a sustainable edge over competitors. Even if you have one today, it could be gone tomorrow. Your prospects can easily locate a whole slew of options from which to choose. While you're told to "sell value," you're not even sure what makes your products or service so darn special. The truth is, they're not.

There's only one thing that truly can be special and that's YOU! That's why one of the SNAP Rules is Be iNvaluable. Absolutely no one can replicate you—your knowledge, your expertise, your problem-solving capability, or your ability to create new options that didn't exist before.

Remember, your prospects can get your products, software, or services anywhere, and probably for much cheaper.

But they can't buy your brain, your knowledge, or your expertise anyplace else. When you focus on turning yourself into the differentiator, suddenly everything shifts. People who wouldn't give you the time of day before suddenly can't get enough of you. They rely on your know-how, guidance, and advice for achieving their goals.

Frazzled customers lack time to think, research, strategize, or reflect. Their frenetic schedules have them racing nonstop from one meeting to the next. They're so busy that they look for resources they can count on: people who are invaluable. If you want to succeed in sales, this needs to be you.

Developing Your Expertise

Believe it or not, when I started my professional career, I never wanted to be in sales. I thought salespeople were slimy, pushy, and self-serving. But after teaching high school for a few years, I came up with a great idea for a service business. In fact, it was so good that I knew it would sell itself. However, the good people at the Service Corps of Retired Executives (SCORE) quickly set my thinking straight.

Based on their advice, I reluctantly entered this profession. But I was not a natural salesperson. I detested everything about it. Pitching, objection handling, closing, and negotiating—it all felt wrong. If I was going to be successful, it wasn't going to be through "traditional" sales skills. Instead, I learned about my prospects' businesses. I focused on asking good questions. I experimented with how to increase engagement, interest, and buy-in. And it worked. I was highly successful—even in my first year.

Fast-forward five years. Instead of selling copiers, I was now selling computer systems—which was a real stretch, since technology overwhelms me. The minute someone starts talking about mash-ups, cloud computing, or configurable agents, my eyes glaze over. Yet I became the International Rookie of the Year for a technology company.

How could that happen? Since it was obvious that my technical know-how would never win me any awards, I focused on what I could become an expert on: the application of that technology to the business environment. I only cared about what difference the technology could make to customers. My entire sales approach focused on that, and when it was time for an in-depth technology conversation, I'd bring in the tech experts.

Amazingly enough, many of my consulting clients over the past twenty years have been high-tech firms. I jokingly tell people that I work with companies who "love their technology too much." But what I bring them is the ability to find and sell the business case buried in their gobbledygook.

Why am I telling you all this? Because expertise is developed over time. It's not something you are born with; it's learned. But it doesn't take forever. In the above examples, I developed a good enough working expertise in very short order to achieve significant success.

Remember, frazzled customers want to work with experts. Fortunately, they don't demand perfection. They do, however, expect you to have a strong working knowledge of what's important to them, and the ability to carry on an intelligent conversation. Your credibility is contingent upon it.

Just because you don't have a wealth of expertise today is no reason not to immediately start working on it. That's why you need to immerse yourself when you're new to a field and why you need to keep on learning throughout your career.

How One Failing Salesperson Became iNvaluable

When Bill moved into his sales position at a printing firm where he'd worked for years, he thought it would be easy. But after leaving 2,500-plus voice mails, he found himself failing fast. That's when he decided to quit selling "printing." After reviewing a variety of projects his company had done over the years, he decided to become a menu expert.

With that new identity, Bill immersed himself in the restaurant industry. He learned the lingo, studied the history, analyzed how big restaurant chains worked, examined their challenges, and read everything he could on menus.

Then he targeted the companies he wanted to land as clients. As he studied their menus, he discovered ways that he could help the restaurants improve them, possibly in ways they'd not yet perceived. Finally, he unleashed his carefully crafted e-mail campaign directly on the chief marketing officers (CMOs) of these big restaurant chains.

Bill discovered that while he was talking to the top marketing person about energizing offers and driving revenue with newly designed menus, his competitors were fighting over price with the supply chain people.

He followed the trade press to identify potential opportunities for new menu sales. He looked for chains that were lowering their prices, expanding into new markets, announcing new menu offerings, and more. When he noticed these trigger events, he'd get in touch. All his communications included strong value propositions with statistics, up-to-date commentary about a restaurant's current direction, and fresh new ideas about how he could help.

The results? In just two years, Bill's company has printed over two million menus for the country's best-known restaurants. He's in active discussions with his top one hundred targeted restaurants. He's blowing out his sales numbers—and having more fun than ever before. And he's expanding his expertise into his next target market right now—but I'm sworn to secrecy and can't reveal it.

Tap into Your MVP Talents

By immersing yourself in any topic—whether it's developing your business acumen or focusing on your presentation skills—you'll quickly become more knowledgeable and proficient than 80 percent of your colleagues.

But you also have talents, passions, and abilities that are part of your personal success equation. When you use them to their fullest, you become an MVP (Most Valuable Player) to your customers. Here are just a few examples of the MVP talents I've seen at work:

- Erin's interest in emerging marketplace trends enables her to continually feed her customers with new ideas to drive sales.
- Raoul's customers benefit from his passion for engineering. He understands their processes, helps them troubleshoot problems, and brings them fresh insights.

- Stacia sees numbers. She's constantly tracking and measuring results and is always looking for ways to help her customers improve productivity.
- Terry builds incredible alliance relationships between organizations that could benefit from working together.
- Doug is an excellent negotiator. He's at his happiest working on complex, multiyear contracts that require him to find creative ways to make the deal work for both parties.

It's important to realize that what we like to do is something we should do more of in the workplace. It's where our personal value resides. If we find a subject interesting, we spend more time learning it, thus further expanding our expertise. In this way we become even more valuable to our customers.

Are you playing to your strengths? Pay attention to what captures your attention or captivates your thinking. Notice what you invest time learning about—even in your leisure time. This is either a current strength or an emerging one. Play to your strengths and interests, and things will become much easier.

After you develop your expertise, the next step is to learn how to leverage it effectively when you're with customers.

21

iNvaluable: Using Your Smarts to Create Change

Notice, we're still talking about the SNAP Factor of iNvaluable. Expertise is only half the equation. Now your challenge is to leverage your personal expertise, and that of your company, to help your prospects understand the value they'd get from making a change. Again, I'm not talking about investing time with just any prospect. That's a big waste.

Our focus is on potential customers who are in your target market. They have similar objectives, issues, and needs as your existing clients. Better yet, they've undergone a triggering event that makes them an even more viable candidate for your offering. You have good reason to suspect you can make a big difference for them. It's on that premise that we move forward.

In *The Experience Economy*, authors Joseph Pine and James Gilmore state that, "Those businesses [sellers] that relegate themselves to the diminishing world of goods and services will be rendered irrelevant. To avoid this fate, you must learn to stage a rich, compelling experience."

Hmmm. An interesting thought. We know that anyone who's suffering from Frazzled Customer Syndrome thinks it's a waste of time to learn about your product or service. The big question then becomes, "What makes an experience with you rich and compelling?"

These "experiences" don't just happen serendipitously. They're created by sellers who recognize the shift that's taken place in the market, who focus on developing their expertise, and who invest time learning about their prospects' business problems. (Like you!)

When these savvy sellers meet with prospective customers, they bring along ideas and insights into business improvement strategies and what's happening in the marketplace with their prospects' customers or their competitors. In short, they get their prospects' thinking.

Pine and Gilmore also say that customers should pay for this "experience." Think about it. Would your prospects willingly pay $500 for an hour of your time? If not, we've got some work to do.

Creating That $500 Customer Experience

Your job is to orchestrate these rich and compelling experiences whenever you connect with prospective customers. You can't leave it up to happenstance. To truly engage your prospects and get them to consider a change initiative, you need to stop winging it and start creating it.

First, kiss your PowerPoints goodbye. Sorry. I know you love having them handy, and sometimes your prospects even request them. But when you do these presentations, you're boring. Incredibly and undeniably boring. PowerPoints turn most sellers into mindless drones who read bullet points verbatim while their prospects zone out. The PowerPoint presentation has become a crutch that gets in the way of your connecting with customers, getting inside their business challenges, establishing your value, and moving them off the status quo.

Instead, you need to replace your unprepared chatter and PowerPoint presentations with compelling conversations, designed by you. Here are several strategies I've used or helped my clients implement that work exceptionally well to create the $500 customer experience.

"I Understand Your Challenge" Strategy

For many years, I specialized in creating sales tools and training that helped companies shorten time to revenue on new product introductions. Initially, it was hard for me to explain my offering without getting dragged down into all the details. But I did notice that my prospects "got it" whenever I used a "throw it over the wall" metaphor to explain the problems created at product launch time due to the division between Sales and Marketing.

So I commissioned a cartoonist to create a graphic I could use when meeting with clients. At the beginning of our conversation, I'd pull out this cartoon to explain to my prospects what I did. My entire focus was on the issues that my customers typically dealt with and the ramifications they had on the success of their new product launch.

By using this approach, my prospects immediately realized that I'd worked with other clients who had similar issues and that I really knew my stuff. Before long, they'd say, "Are you sure you haven't worked for our company before?"

When I heard that, I knew we were now on the same team. I

was no longer selling to them. Instead, guided by my preplanned questions, they willingly shared information with me about the issues they'd faced at launch time and about upcoming product launches. Before I knew it, we were setting up a follow-up meeting and I was ensuring that the right people were there.

By finding a creative way to demonstrate how you help your prospects solve their problems, you can really speed up your sales cycle. One of my clients, who worked in the heart valve industry, created a small quartz "vein" to show physicians how blood flows in the human body. This simple tool highlighted why the design of his company's valve was so much more effective—and immediately boosted sales.

"Closing the Gap" Strategy

This is another strategy you can use to engage your prospects in the $500 conversation. The purpose of this exercise is to help your prospects identify where they are today, where they want to be, and what needs to be done to get them there. Your job is to be the facilitator, the person who's simply trying to get all the relevant information out on the table so that it can be addressed or considered.

The discussion you lead will center on a diagram that you'll draw on a flip chart or white board. At the top left, write "Today"; on the top right, "Future." Then draw a cloud in between and write "Gap" inside it. Remain standing—even if you don't have to. All eyes will be on you, and it may be a bit uncomfortable, but you need to be the leader.

Start out by saying, "In order for me to see if we'll be able to [insert value proposition], we need to talk about where you are today and what your objectives are in the upcoming twelve months. So if you don't mind, let's start with today. Can you tell me more about your status quo?" Whatever information they give you, write it down in bullet points under the "Today" column head. If you don't get a lot of insight, prompt your prospects with additional questions. Using questions to direct the focus of the meeting is one of the best ways to demonstrate your knowledge.

Then, you repeat the same process regarding their desired future state. Finally, you tackle the "gap" by asking questions such as, "What have you done already? How's that working for you? What else needs to be addressed for you to achieve your objectives?"

You can use this "closing the gap" strategy at the beginning of your conversation as a structure for the questions you want to ask. Or you can use it when you're in a meeting where dozens of opinions are flying around and things are getting a little confusing. This is particularly effective if you have a group of people in the room. It helps keep the focus on what's important to their business and what's solvable by your offering.

Prospects typically become very engaged in these discussions. Another benefit of this strategy is that it gets the people in the company talking among themselves. It's amazing how many different ideas and perspectives come out. They leave the meeting feeling that it's been a high-value use of their time and that they've had a chance to give their input.

"Mind Expansion" Strategy

One of the biggest challenges in selling is expanding people's thinking. Sometimes they have a limited perception of the factors affecting their ability to reach their goals.

As an example, I recently met with a company that was struggling with new customer acquisition. For years, their existing client's growth and strong relationships had kept their own revenues moving up. But when the economy soured, they recognized that something needed to change, but they weren't sure what to do.

Training was an option. While we did talk about that, I made sure they understood that there were other issues they needed to address. To make this concept more tangible, I used a white board to create a mind map, diagramming the various sales issues they were concerned with as we spoke, then facilitated a discussion on each of the points made.

The result? The exercise cemented my expertise as a sales strategist who could help their salespeople now, but also provided valuable guidance on the other issues they needed to tackle.

"Show and Don't Tell Too Much" Strategy

In some industries, sellers have many "show-and-tell" items they can use to showcase their products or services. This plethora of options actually hinders their ability to get the business. That's why I developed this strategy. Here are two different examples to highlight how it might be used.

Client A sold face masks to companies concerned with occupational health and environmental safety. Every meeting with a safety director began with "Show me whatcha got new." After quickly perusing the new item, the safety director would then ask, "How much?" Whatever the price, it was always too high.

I worked with this client on a major product launch—one where they were introducing "revolutionary new technologies." They hoped to leverage this to grow market share and combat the commoditization mentality.

So this time we chose to do something different. Rather than sending the reps out with the finished face masks, they brought with them a technology sample kit that included the new nose clips, fibers, and air valves. This gave the reps the opportunity to expand on the value of these major enhancements. The result? One month later, when the new product line was officially introduced, they realized significant growth.

> Client B is really a composite of the many companies I've worked for who sell promotional ideas, direct mail, branding, collateral, packaging, coupons, graphics, event exhibits, and more to marketing departments. They could show samples all day long and still not run out of cool things with which to impress their customers. "And then we did this project . . . and this one . . . and this one."

Sellers love this because it's so much fun to show all their goodies. Prospects love seeing what they've done because it expands their own thinking. But often it leads to nothing, so here's what I suggest. Pick out one to three (max) sample projects to show. Then, when you meet with your prospects, say, "I've brought along several samples to show you that are reflective of our work. I also have a number of questions regarding your initiative and direction. So, if you don't mind, I'd like to start there. Can you tell me what was the driving force behind your desire to change?"

After you've asked the questions you feel are important, then you might say, "Thanks for the background. It helps me put into context what I'm going to show you. For example, this project was developed for a client who was facing a similar challenge in the marketplace. Their goal was to [explain their goal]. Here's what we did for them [show project] and these are the results they attained . . ."

This enables you to show your best projects at the same time you have a business-focused conversation that's highly relevant to your prospect.

"I Understand Your Challenge," "Closing the Gap," "Mind Expansion," and "Show and Don't Tell Too Much" are just four strategies I've helped sellers use to create value even before they earn the customers' business. They leverage the seller's knowledge and skills about the business. More important, they engage customers in a business-oriented dialogue from the get-go.

I've seen technical sellers pull out process flow diagrams and map how things flow through an organization. Their focus is on the places where things typically go wrong. I've seen other sellers draw the silos between departments and the multiple handoff points as they discuss the tremendous inefficiencies in departments.

What's important to realize is what these graphics, diagrams, and handouts are *not*. They are not PowerPoint slides. They're not brochures. They are not marketing collateral. They are not four-color glossies. They're black-and-white printouts at their fanciest. And, most often, they're just your drawings.

That's their power, because now the focus of the meeting isn't on your product, service, or solution. It's on your customers' most important challenges.

The people you're meeting with are not passive observers and evaluators. You're collaborating with them on a subject near and dear to their hearts: their business, their challenges, their objectives. You're building a relationship with them, helping them, and demonstrating your ability to be a significant contributor to their business improvement process.

Do you have any idea how irresistible this is? Give it a try and you'll never go back to your PowerPoints again.

22

iNvaluable: Be an Everyday Value Creator

I f your prospects are complacent, it may take them a while to commit to change. Because of this, you'll have multiple interactions with the people involved in making the decision before it's actually made. It's your job to help them discover if it makes good business sense to move ahead, and help them see possibilities they've never considered before.

Remember that these frazzled people are looking for a smart, savvy business partner whose expertise they can trust. In their world of everyday chaos, they often lack the mental bandwidth for strategic thinking, keeping on top of trends, or knowing what competitors are doing. That's why, if you become an everyday value creator, you will stand out.

So stop thinking about getting the order and start thinking of yourself as a business improvement specialist whose product/ service is only one part of the value you bring to your potential and current customers.

You need to bring your prospects ideas, insights, and information from the beginning of your relationship. Anytime you help them understand their problems in greater depth or bring them innovative approaches to achieve their business objectives, you'll endear yourself to these crazy-busy people. Let's take a look now at some more ways you can be iNvaluable.

Stimulate Your Prospects' Thinking

You already know that if you ask questions, your prospects will see you as more competent and caring, but you may not realize that some questions are better than others.

Plain vanilla questions such as "What are your objectives for the coming year?" or "What are your primary problems?" can be asked by any reasonably trained seller without much knowledge or experience.

However, if you want to get to the Go Zone, you need to take your questioning skills to a whole new level. More specific questions demonstrate your expertise in the subtlest yet most effective ways, and your prospects won't answer them with their usual "I have a salesperson in my office" voice.

Instead, they will stop in their tracks to reflect on what you've just asked. They'll need to analyze, compare, contrast, assess, create, synthesize, and evaluate. Not only do you get valuable information from these questions, but you also get big-time respect.

Nick Miller, author of *Winning at Prospecting*, warns sellers about asking "rookie questions" and says that "more prepared questions are interesting, worth discussion; they dig at subtleties and challenges that keep decision makers up at night."

Over the years, I've discovered that "wrapping" questions with information that shows your knowledge or provides context will significantly enhance your success rate. Not only do you gather information from your prospect's response, but you establish yourself as an expert. It's not hard to do either—if you think about it ahead of time.

When I first started my career at Xerox, I began asking a simple question that set me apart from other sellers: "Mr. Prospect, in working with other companies who were making copier decisions, I find that they're typically concerned with four very basic criteria: ease of operation, flexibility, reliability, and quality. Can you tell me which of these factors is most important to you and why?"

See how I brought in my experience? My company told me those factors were important to customers, so I leveraged their expertise. You can do that, too.

Since you're researching companies or individuals prior to a meeting, you can also leverage the information you uncover. For example, you might say:

> I see that your company is planning to introduce multiple new products in the upcoming months. I also notice that you're consolidating your channel partners at the same time. What are your plans for driving sales of these new systems at the same time you're shrinking the number of feet on the street?

Or, you might ask:

> In my work with other VPs of Sales, a key challenge I've found they face is improving sales force productivity. I've seen multiple initiatives to address this issue—training,

sales tool development, leveraging Sales 2.0 resources, lead generation programs, and more. What has your company done so far in this area and how would you assess its effectiveness in light of today's business environment?

These direct and thoughtful questions pull together disparate pieces of information and get people thinking about new things. Prospects find them refreshing and stimulating, and thus they think better of you. Whenever you can, wrap your questions with what you've uncovered in your research, your work with other companies, or your industry knowledge.

Be a Business Improvement Specialist

Because most sellers believe their appeal is all about their product, service, or solution, they totally miss the myriad ways in which they can bring value to people who are willing to consider a change.

Let me give you an example of what you could do to create value—even if you sell something that's essentially a commodity. As you read these ideas, think about how they relate to what you offer.

Let's say you sell direct mail programs. You could create value for crazy-busy buyers by showing them how to reduce the overall cost of the program while maintaining its effectiveness and integrity. You could share relevant information regarding "best practices" and what your company has learned from working with similar organizations. You could inform them about what their competitors are doing, industry trends, and how other companies are capitalizing on changes in the field. You could suggest ways for them to improve their database or their project flow and handoffs.

All these areas of value creation are within the capabilities of the individual seller—someone like you! They're all about business improvement, not pitching your offering. They're all things you can learn about by immersing yourself in your customer's business and industry.

These value-creation strategies help your prospects open themselves up to your ideas. Plus, they help them recognize that their status quo isn't perfect, or that it's even more imperfect than they've assumed. And finally, these strategies help your prospects solidify the decision to move to a better option—hopefully one that includes you.

Challenge Your Prospects' Perspectives

When was the last time you made your prospects really stop and think? If you're just spouting self-serving sales talk, the answer is probably never. But if you've developed personal expertise, you probably have a better chance of rocking your prospects' boat.

I'm not talking about being a know-it-all who one-ups everyone. Nor am I talking about being a boorish churl who drones on endlessly. When you have expertise and want to provoke your prospects' thinking, you have to approach them as if you were in their service—helping them achieve their goals. In the previous chapter, you learned strategies you can use in meetings to get people thinking. But there are so many other ways that provocation can be used—especially when your prospects' perspectives are limited to their own experiences or worldview.

For example, recently Nina Millhouse, who sells into the hospital industry, made a gutsy move. She challenged her prospects' thinking with a study done by a big accounting firm:

> In today's ailing economy, when every dollar counts, hospitals are looking for ways to improve their bottom line. One option is to add $11.7 million in revenue. The other option is to reduce operating costs by $100,000. According to Deloitte and Touche, these two options have the same impact, but clearly one is more achievable. That's what I want to talk with you about today.

Now that's a jolt! She knew her prospects might consider her offering "trivial" in light of all the other crises facing hospitals today. So she shared a new way of looking at what she could do for them by comparing the top line revenue growth needed to match the $100,000 savings she could deliver.

Don't be afraid to tell your prospects when you think they're making a mistake. Sometimes when my prospects tell me what they're doing to achieve their objectives, a little indicator light goes off in my head that says, "Huh? That doesn't seem quite right." In the past I'd let it go, thinking perhaps I'd missed something or didn't understand. Now I always speak up—but often very gently, even if I know they're wrong. I don't ever want a prospect to feel stupid or embarrassed. Nor do I want to come barreling at them like a bull in a china shop. That only makes people more defensive of what they're doing. So, I might say something like:

> Eric, I know that your primary strategy to drive new customer acquisition this year is to get your salespeople to

make more calls. I'd like to challenge your thinking on that a bit. My experience in working with sales teams across the country shows me that the quality of the call has far more effect on success than the quantity. In fact, if you really want to have a significant impact, your salespeople need to have easy access to sales intelligence tools. Can you tell me what you're doing in this area?

More often than not, these gentle provocations open the door to an interesting dialogue that enables me to make suggestions, offer advice, and provide guidance—nicely, and as a potential partner who cares about their success.

Provocation is particularly important to use when your prospects currently don't have money in their budget for your product or service. Whether you offer a contrarian perspective, fresh insights, new visions of the future, or missing information, it helps crazy-busy buyers see beyond the status quo to what is possible.

So there you have it. Three full chapters on how you can be iNvaluable during the second decision. I hope you've learned how, when you focus on being invaluable, you can literally create new sales opportunities out of thin air. Remember, I'm not saying you should do this with every sales call you make. These strategies work best when you focus on targeted businesses who have similar objectives and/or challenges as your best customers.

Frazzled customers are looking for someone to lead them out of their everyday chaos. Being an everyday value creator enables that to happen. Now you just need to make it simple for them to change—which just happens to be what we'll look at next.

23

Simple: Cut the Complexity

I know it's an odd thing to say, but complacency has its advantages. Just ask any prospect who is quite content to stay with their status quo and avoid the extra work involved in change. But the moment you introduce the possibility of a better future into prospects' worldview, you force them to wake up and make choices. Do they stick their head in the sand and ignore your ideas, insights, and information because change is just too much work? Or do they invest time learning more about how to better achieve their objectives?

The stronger your business case is, the more likely your prospects will move forward with a decision to change. The more you've allowed them to see "what's possible," the harder it is to turn back. But the real work has only just begun—and your prospects know it.

From their vantage point, they see endless meetings ahead of them. They realize that their recommendations must withstand

executive scrutiny. They need to be able to justify the use of corporate funds, address potential risks, and ensure implementation success. They're also very aware of how a stupid decision
can derail their career. All this is working against you.

Yet if you've piqued your prospects' curiosity enough, they'll
make a change. Conceptual buy-in is the first step in moving
them away from the status quo—and bravo to you when you've
achieved it.

But now your prospects need to learn more. If it's their first
time making a decision in this area, they'll need to understand
the entire context of the change initiative. If it's been a few years
since their previous decision, they'll also need to do a major
immersion.

The sheer challenge of figuring it all out is daunting. And it
gets even more overwhelming as your prospects see just how
much they don't know. That's why it's imperative to always follow SNAP Rule 1: "Keep It Simple."

It's Time to Play "Follow the Leader"

What happens to frazzled prospects at this point? Many of them
quit. They throw their arms up in total frustration and become
overwhelmed. They tell you, "What you're talking about sounds
really good, but there's just not enough time to do the necessary
due diligence. We need to put it on the back burner for at least
the next three to four months."

If this happens, you're toast. You've been consigned to the
D-Zone even though your ideas are aligned with their direction
and you provide significant business value. You've been stopped
by the complexity of change. Because your prospects can't handle

it, they'll put you off until some future time when they hope life will be easier. It'll never happen.

To be successful with today's crazy-busy customers, you must lead with simplicity. And you must do it *before* your prospects hit this crisis point.

As marketing expert Britton Manasco says on his Illuminating the Future blog, "They [customers] lack the knowledge, evidence, experience, trust and confidence necessary to invest and commit. More than anything, they are seeking reliable guidance that will give them the confidence to move successfully forward. No one likes change, of course. But no one likes standing still—and being left behind—either."

If you're reading this book, you want better sales results. You want direction. You want someone to tell you, "Pay attention to this, because it's important" or "The next thing you need to do is . . ." Your prospects want the same from you. They want you to use your expertise to guide them through the complex decision-making process. They want to feel they're in the competent hands of a person who's helped other companies achieve breakthrough results.

It's time to be the leader, the guide, the navigator. Once you've captured your prospects' attention, you need to move into this new role. In a figurative sense, you offer them your hand and say, "Follow me. I can help you figure this out and get it implemented in your organization. I've done it before. C'mon, let's go." When you do this, frazzled customers will follow you.

Illuminate the Path Forward

Josh Braun, vice-president of business development at Jellyvision, knows how to simplify decisions for his prospects. He's very strategic about targeting companies where he believes his company's services can make a significant difference. He leverages business intelligence to identify the best entry point and positioning for his account entry campaign.

In his initial meetings, he engages his prospects by showing a strong ROI business case and demo samples specifically chosen because of their relevance to his prospects' situation.

Once he has their interest and attention, he deliberately slows things down—most often in a follow-up meeting. He'll say, "If this is something you're really interested in, let's go over the critical pieces you need to consider in order to get successful results."

At this point, he'll walk them through documents such as the "Steps in Our Process" and a "Client Resource Overview." He also details his company's and the client's responsibilities in the development and implementation of the customized solution.

This typically elicits responses such as "Oh, we didn't realize . . ." or "We'll need to get Christine involved . . ." This opens the conversation to everything that needs to be considered as they move forward, including who needs to be involved, the decisions that need to be made, and possible time frames.

Ultimately, by sharing this process, Braun strengthens his relationship with his prospects and demonstrates his competence, and his firm's. Moving forward, they turn to him for advice, with questions such as "What do we do next?" "How do you handle . . . ?" and "What if this happens?"

Of course, there's a downside. Sometimes deals fall apart because the prospects can't handle the amount of work required on their side. But Josh uncovers this early on, instead of after months of work. If there's a danger of this, he puts them on his list of prospects to nurture and keeps in touch with them on a regular basis.

But look at the upside. He's leading, showing his prospects the path forward. He's simplifying everything for them—saving them hundreds of hours trying to figure it out themselves. They want this help. They value this guidance. They look to him for answers.

Candid Conversations About the Tough Stuff

Getting conceptual buy-in is the important first step. But you're a long way from that commitment to change. You need to help your prospects deal with the challenges they'll inevitably face as they sell your proposed business improvement idea internally.

You need to address these issues up front—unflinchingly. There's nothing harder than bringing up these potentially show-stopping obstacles. Believe me, I too have shuddered over doing it. But amazingly enough, your forthrightness in raising these issues actually minimizes them at the same time that it enhances your expertise.

The key is to detach yourself from your desire to sell right now. That's hard to do when you know your prospects like your ideas. But to really help them achieve their goals—and ultimately sell your product or service—you have to face the tough stuff and facilitate that important discussion.

When I did product launch consulting, I sometimes entered into companies through Marketing; other times I came in through Sales. But I always had to ask about:

Funding: I know that you really like this idea, but what is it going to take to get budget approval for this project? What projects are currently less important than this one?

Engagement: Besides you and your marketing/sales counterpart, who else needs to be involved in this decision-making process?

"Not Invented Here" Syndrome: Who's not going to be happy with this change initiative? What issues are we facing?

Often, I would end these questions with a statement such as this: "My experience shows me that we need to . . . , but every organization has its own unique way of doing things. So what are your thoughts on this?"

By bringing up these subjects, you simplify your prospects' decision making. You're telling them who needs to be involved and what needs to be talked about. Now they know what to do. They don't have to research it themselves. You've made it easy for them.

Buying Facilitation® Questions

In *Dirty Little Secrets*, Sharon Drew Morgen recommends getting the "Buying Team" assembled as early as possible, since it makes it so much easier for your prospects to move forward quickly. Here are several questions she recommends asking:

- Have you ever done anything like this before? If so, how did you find the right people to involve? And what, from that process, can you use here? If not, what would you need to consider to help your internal folks know that something like we're suggesting would support your business objectives?

- At what point would you recognize all the past initiatives, departments, and vendors that have maintained your status quo and would need to buy in to change in order for you to move forward?
- Once the Buying Team is fully formed, what would you need to be considering given your status quo to know how to move forward in such a way that you don't meet resistance?
- And how could you all move together, one step at a time, so that you could create a workable plan in a manageable time scale?
- What would you need to see from me to help you get where you need to be? And at what point would you need me to support your internal buy-in efforts?

Not your typical sales questions, are they? Morgen's research shows that using these facilitative-type questions can slash your sales cycles significantly. You're not pushing your prospects forward; you're guiding them to make the best decision for their organization, at the same time that you make things easier for them. The best thing about it is that your unbiased guidance increases your own perceived value. You become the trusted adviser, the go-to resource your prospects turn to when questions arise or expertise is needed.

Go back and read those questions again. Right now. Think about them. They're what a project manager would ask. That's the mind-set you need. Then look at the issues you typically run into and create your own questions to simplify the complexity for your prospects.

Make Everything Easier

Here are some strategies to make things easier for frazzled customers. Remember, people hate complexity. It's an anti–SNAP Factor. You want to eliminate it everywhere.

Augment, Don't Replace.

Your prospects already use something (vendor, internal/external resource) to address their needs. It's always easier for them to add on to an existing program, process, or technology than to justify something entirely new.

For example, when I talk to VPs of Sales, I always stress that my workshops on selling to crazy-busy customers or cracking into corporate accounts complement their existing sales training initiatives. In fact, since I'm familiar with most of the popular programs, I'll even assure them that I'll tie my strategies in with their current methodology.

Recently I sold a prospect conceptually on a new way to bring much-needed services to an underserved customer demographic. To make the decision easier, I showed them how we'd leverage outside resources to jump-start the new program and then turn it over to their own internal staff.

Think about how you can coexist with what your prospects are currently doing to address their needs. You could have a battle on your hands if you try to replace an external vendor. Or, if it's an internal resource, you may face an insurrection.

Think and Act Small.

If your prospects like your idea, they'll want to get it approved as soon as possible. However, big ideas with big budgets are riskier and require more buy-in. As a result, they're harder to get through the system.

So even if you have a big idea, be realistic with your prospects. Talk about starting small. Show them how you can get started, demonstrate your success, and build from there. For example, you could:

- Propose an initial assessment to understand the scope of the problem.
- Tackle a small problem where you could demonstrate immediate short-term results.
- Focus on bringing in just one of your products, services, or solutions.
- Suggest a change in only one of the departments or a single facility.

IT seller P. V. Bhaskar proposes pilot projects to his clients. With a 90 percent conversion rate, they've become his secret weapon to simplify the decision making. Prior to getting started, he allows the CIO and CFO to set the success parameters. As he says, "When a pilot exceeds the incumbent's performance, all I need to do is demonstrate that the success can be scaled to an actual project as well."

Going for the whole shebang at once makes things more difficult. And when you're working with frazzled customers, that's a setup for being consigned to the dreaded D-Zone. But once you get your foot in the door, the hardest part is over. If you do a good job on your initial piece of business, it will be logical for your prospect to move to the next stage with your company.

Root Out All Complexity.

Because of our chaotic business environments, simplicity has recently emerged as a key factor in sales success. You're dealing not only with overwhelmed, stressed-out decision makers but also with people who don't make decisions like this often.

In many cases, your prospects don't know what to look for or how to decide. If things get complicated, they'll quit and you'll be gonzo. That's why it's imperative for you and your company to ask these questions all the time:

- At which point do our prospects tip into overwhelm?
- What are the complexities that grind decisions to a halt?
- How can we reduce the ease and effort needed to make a decision?
- In what ways can we minimize decision-making risk?

Discuss these questions with your colleagues. Observe what happens in conversations with your prospects. Talk to your existing customers to get their feedback. You need to focus on rooting out all complexity, because it's a major showstopper. Simplicity is your ultimate goal.

24

Priorities:
Maintain the Momentum

After you've convinced your prospects of the need for change, you'll need to keep the momentum going to encourage the decision-making process. Even after you've brought them a solid idea—one that addresses a critical problem or achieves their objectives—things can get bogged down.

We've already talked about the need to keep things simple and lead your prospects through the complexities of the decision-making process. You have to keep it simple, eliminating as many of the difficulties as you can. You also need to work collaboratively with your prospects to build a strong business case with a solid ROI or short payback time. Having a financial urgency keeps the decision a top priority.

Still, there are times when your prospects disappear into the proverbial "black hole" never to be seen again. At first, you assume their lack of responsiveness is an isolated event. But after repeated failed attempts to connect, you start to question your sanity. You could have sworn they were interested, but their current behavior indicates otherwise. Not wanting to appear too desperate or to come across as a pest, you're uncertain of what your next steps should be. After a few "check-in" phone calls and offers to help out in any way you can, you wonder what to do next.

According to Ken Rudin, entrepreneur and sales analytics expert, "As deals get older, they lose momentum, and that translates into a significantly lower probability of winning the deal. What this means is that after a certain amount of time, if you haven't yet won a deal, you need to re-qualify the opportunity to see if it's still viable, or determine if you're wasting your time."

This is true even if your prospects loved your idea and thought it would provide phenomenal impact for their company. Unfortunately, it doesn't take long for the urgency to wear off after you leave the scene. Life happens, priorities shift, and everyday firefighting takes precedence.

Even in the face of such challenges, it's your responsibility to keep things moving. Even when your prospects disappear into the black hole, you need to keep the decision at the forefront of their minds and provide them assistance in getting away from the status quo.

TMTQ: Avoiding Information Overload

The best way to accelerate your prospects' decision-making process and keep it a priority is to remove those factors that bog it down. People don't want to make slow decisions. However, they don't want to make dumb, career-derailing decisions, either.

George Silverman, author of *The Secrets of Word-of-Mouth Marketing*, says "Your competitors, trade publications and other information sources are flooding the customer with information.

But usually, the more information the customer gets, the more indecisive he is."

Information overload paralyzes people. And many sellers don't realize just how much they contribute to this problem. Wanting to keep things moving along, they overwhelm their prospects with every conceivable bit of knowledge at their disposal. It's eagerness. It's excitement. It's the thrill of a hot prospect, combined with the need to close the business.

It's the urge to do TMTQ: "Too much, too quickly." When you surprise your prospects with all the informational resources at your disposal, they can't handle it. Instead of speeding up your sales process, it boomerangs on you and slows everything down. The additional complexity derails the momentum, perhaps even sending you into the dreaded D-zone.

How to Speed Up Decisions

Remember, the second decision is all about getting complacent prospects to act. In order to do this, you have to make sure they have the appropriate information to help them through the decision-making process. I'm talking about solid educational content that addresses whatever issue they're hung up on. Think substance, not slickness.

That means you need to identify all their potential sticking points. Do it from your prospects' point of view, not yours. Use their words, the way they'd say it. Get them all out. That's the only way to deal with them.

Then, once you've created that list of sticking points, put on your thinking cap to figure out what type of educational content you can create or leverage to move them through these decision bottlenecks. The following chart details numerous ideas you can use.

PROSPECT'S ISSUE	MOMENTUM-BUILDING TOOLS
We don't see any reason to change.	• Articles on relevant industry trends, fresh ways of looking at traditional problems • White papers on challenges facing organizations today, future forecasts, or emerging business models • Assessment tools to determine if costly problems or missed opportunities exist • Interviews with industry experts and thought leaders
We're not sure if it's worth it.	• Case studies featuring clients before/after scenarios • White papers on the business case for change • Benchmark tools to enable comparisons • ROI, total cost of ownership, and payback analysis tools to determine value in making a change
We can't figure out how it would work here.	• Examples of how other customers use your products or services • Demonstrations to offer initial proof of concept
We're concerned how it would impact how we're currently doing things.	• Map of steps involved in process detailing decisions to be made, who needs to be involved, and choice points • List of key factors to consider in making the change • Conversations with others who have gone through change process • Lessons learned and tricks of the trade
Is this for real? Are others doing it?	• Papers or studies by industry experts and analysts regarding importance of change in today's business climate • Video testimonials of customers detailing the value they've received
We're struggling to get buy-in.	• List of tough questions that need to be addressed by group before moving ahead • Peer-level meetings with teams from your organization and your prospects • Interview with individual leading the change initiative in a similar company

Assemble Your Own Tool Kit

Right now, you may be worried that you don't have a lot of momentum-building tools. Ideally, your company would create them for you. But if they don't—or if you work for yourself—it's imperative to develop your own. You can also leverage other people's content if it supports your prospects' educational needs or hire a content creator to help you get started.

Don't think you have to create every one of these items. They're just suggestions. You need to figure out what educational content will have the highest impact for your particular prospects.

One woman I know has just started working for a top-notch consulting firm. Business was great during boom times. But when the economy took a downturn, suddenly she needed these sales tools to help prospects justify spending so much on their solution. Right now her primary focus is on getting case studies she can use. After that, she's tackling articles on relevant topics.

You do what you have to do. One step a time. Just get started, and before long you'll have multiple tools you can use. They can be written documents such as articles, white papers, checklists, or e-books. They can be assessment tools, or they can leverage other media such as Webinars, seminars, podcasts, or videos.

The less thinking, organizing, researching, deliberating, sorting, evaluating, and assessing your prospects need to do on their own, the better it is for you and for them. Plus, these information-rich sales tools encapsulate all four SNAP Rules. They simplify your prospects' decision making at the same time that they increase your personal value, align with your prospects' business objectives, and keep the decision a priority. Hopefully that's the kick in the butt you need to start assembling your own tool kit.

Provide the Invaluable Resources

The key is to parcel these educational resources out slowly—one at a time. You'll have to resist the urge to pile all the goodies on at once. Instead, you need to identify what you think is causing your prospects' hesitation. Once you've done that, you can send the appropriate resource or link.

Here's what some of your sales-savvy colleagues do to maintain momentum:

- Kimberly Nelson, who works in construction sales, contacts her prospects to point out problems they may encounter and shares alternative ideas. She does this proactively, before they request assistance.
- Nick Wright, an account manager for an Internet technology company, sends quick-hit e-mails that show how other companies are succeeding with the same solution he's proposed to his prospect.
- Tim McDonough, who sells software, suggests getting your prospects' peers and superiors involved if you haven't already done so. Get their input, share your concepts, and deepen your value.

Really savvy salespeople do not "check in" or "touch base." They provide value to prospects with each contact to help encourage a quick decision. It's a strategic and careful process, but it's worth it.

Become the Catalytic Agent

When Justyn Howard, enterprise account manager for Learn. com, identifies prospects with acknowledged needs, he focuses on doing what it takes to turn this opportunity into a reality. Even before his prospects commit to making a change, he's already working with them as if it will happen. For example, he:

- **Engages other stakeholders.** He sets the tone early, making clear that he needs to meet with multiple people, including key decision makers, in order to quantify business impact, prepare presentations, and help them do their job.
- **Brings in resources early.** He introduces his prospects to the implementation team and walks them through the process. This shows his confidence in the solution, increases his prospects' "skin in the game," and helps transfer ownership prior to selection.
- **Involves senior executives.** As soon as he feels he has a 50 percent chance of getting the business, he drafts a stellar letter for his CEO/COO to send his prospects. In it, the executive lets customers know they have the support of the entire organization, from the top down.

Justyn knows how essential it is to follow SNAP Rule 4: Raise Priorities. Everything he does is to maintain momentum and keep the change decision moving along.

Sometimes, if you see that things aren't going the way you want, new strategies are required. Sales executive Jennifer Burman Olson from Savvis offers this advice: "If they haven't seen that your value outweighs the risk of moving off the status quo, you need to either change the game or walk away."

After months of getting high interest in her company's customer service training program, but no sales, that's exactly what key account strategist Catherine McQuaid did. She changed the message and went back to her prospects. This time she focused on improving customer experiences instead of the program details. She called on different decision makers who had a vested interest in this new area. And she emphasized how an investment amplified the financial returns of their previous investments.

The result? A large initial sale to a major financial institution that blossomed into multiple assignments, which then led to contracts with four other big banks.

Don't wait around for your prospect to get in touch with you. Keep thinking of fresh reasons you can get in front of them, bringing them more ideas, insights, and information to help them achieve their desired business outcomes.

The Black Hole Revisited

Despite your best efforts, there are times when nothing you do seems to work. For whatever reason—and there are many—your prospects appear to have decided to stay with the status quo even if it is obviously unwise.

But you don't live in their world. You don't know the pressures they're under. You don't know the turf battles they're fighting. You don't know who is impacted negatively by your proposal and fighting to keep things the same. You don't know their financial situation. And in most cases, you never will. This is information that's privy only to insiders.

So at some point—after eight to ten contacts—you may decide to let them off the hook. Send your prospects an e-mail stating that you thought they were interested, but perhaps you misjudged the situation, since you haven't heard back from them in the last six weeks. Believe it or not, this strategy often gets a response and an explanation from a prospect who is feeling guilty about not reconnecting.

If that doesn't work, reduce your contact frequency. Perhaps you can contact them on a quarterly basis. Or you might want to keep on top of what's happening in the account and reconnect at a more appropriate time. You may not want to give up entirely, though. To many of your prospects, you're their conscience. Every time you call or e-mail them, it's a visible reminder that they need to take action on something that's important to them.

If this still doesn't work, you can walk away. This is not a defeat. Your time is valuable, too, and you need to move on to opportunities that you can win. However, always try to figure out what you might have done differently to get better results.

25

Success with the Second Decision

When you pursue business with a company or an individual who hasn't been thinking about making a change, you take on quite a challenge. To have success with the first decision, you needed to pique the interest of your targeted prospects. Your mission was accomplished when they agreed to an initial meeting.

But working with prospects as they struggle with the second decision is an entirely different matter. It takes strong business acumen, personal expertise, leadership skills, and a lot of street smarts to help someone understand why it's in their best interest to leave the status quo behind.

This challenge is compounded by the fact that you're dealing with frazzled customers who haven't got time for either the pain or the potential gain. Not only that, they often have to mobilize and lead a decision team filled with competing agendas, varying perspectives on their current status, and even more diverse opinions on how to get to their desired objectives.

Yet you manage to unearth problems they didn't know they had, find solutions to their unsolvable issues, and show them how to capitalize on new opportunities.

That's why there are no sweeter words at this time than, "We've decided we need to change."

Sometimes There Is No Third Decision

If you've done all this work, there are times when your prospect will look right at you and say, "Let's get going." This frequently happen to sellers who excel at this stage of the sales process. You see, crazy-busy customers—if they really like your ideas, business value, and personal expertise—don't want to spend time looking at their other options.

They know they want you, your product or service, and your company. Done deal. They may, at times, still have to go through the charade of making the unbiased decision—meaning they call in multiple vendors to get their bids or proposals.

It's likely that you'll still have to write a proposal, prepare a presentation to an executive team, or create a thorough ROI analysis. But you won't be an outsider trying to get in anymore. You'll be working as part of the team.

In fact, you'll start hearing your prospects use the word *we*—as in, "When we kick off this program . . ." or "What else do we need to do . . . ?" That's a great word, *we*. As soon as you hear it, you know that the sale has been made, even though no contract has been signed.

Your role at this time has to shift. You have to stop "selling"— meaning make no pitches at all. You are now working with your customer. So get started by figuring out what to do to make that transition from the status quo. Operate as if you have already started the project.

At the same time, don't lose sight of the fact that the decision could still be derailed, delayed, or even tabled forever. Remember, you haven't signed the contract yet.

It Ain't Over Till It's Over

If you've invested lots of time working with prospects at this phase of the decision-making process, you'll probably feel a bit burned if they insist on looking at other options. After all, you've done the hard work of showing them how they'd benefit from making a change. You deserve the sale.

But sometimes you have to earn the right to your prospect's business all over again as they enter the third decision. At that point, the game changes. They have a whole new agenda. There are new rules, new factors under consideration, new options, and even new players.

On the positive side, all the effort you expended to help your prospects puts you in the best possible position to get their business. You know more about their company, internal workings, goals, strategic initiatives, politics, and people than any of your competitors. You have established relationships and open lines of communications. You're a valuable resource.

Because you've been such an incredible conduit of information, your prospects will seek you out with their questions and concerns. They'll turn to you to help them determine their decision-making criteria. They want to know how other companies have made their selections.

Clearly, this doesn't guarantee that you'll win at the third decision. However, you've set a strong benchmark against which all competitors will be measured. You've:

- Simplified the decision-making process as much as possible;
- Been iNvaluable in providing assistance;
- Aligned yourself with their business objectives; and
- Kept the decision a priority, despite the inevitable pull of the status quo.

You're becoming a true master of working with frazzled prospects. When you follow the SNAP Rules you get more business. Now, on to the third decision.

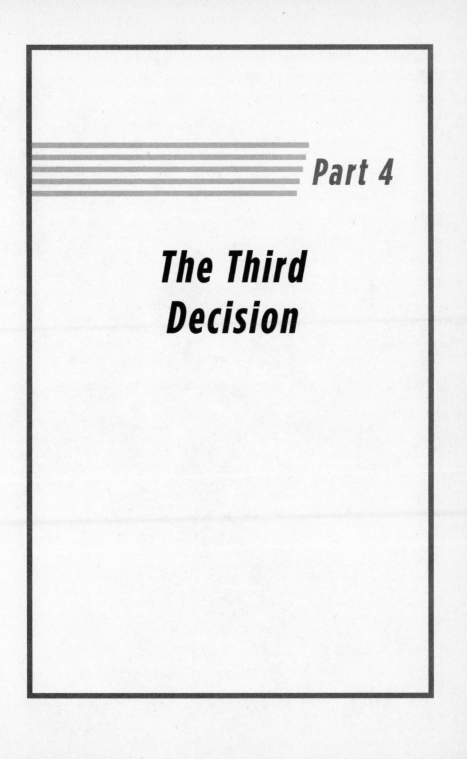

Part 4

The Third Decision

26

Third Decision Overview

Customer's Perspective

By now your prospects have committed to making a change. The status quo is no longer acceptable. They've discovered new ways to eliminate costly problems or to create new opportunities. Now they're looking at what it's going to take to get the approval for change. Here's what these frazzled customers are thinking:

- I'm not sure how to choose; there are so many options.
- I need to be able to justify my choice to the powers that be.
- I'm sticking my neck out; there's a lot of risk in moving forward. I need to minimize it as best I can.
- We'll be living with the results of this decision for a long time, so it better be a good one.

Competition

You have lots of competition—more than you likely suspect:

- The incumbent who, perhaps asleep up until now, will wake up with a vengeance and do whatever it takes to keep their customer.
- Internal resources who would prefer to keep the work in house rather than using an outside company.
- Traditional competitors who are offering products or services very similar to your company's.
- Nontraditional competitors who offer your prospects a totally different way to achieve their objectives.
- Other, more urgent uses of corporate funds that may arise during the evaluation process.

Risks and Fears

Making a bad decision is at the forefront of your prospects' minds. They worry about a chosen company's inability to deliver the promised results, about poor service, and about non-responsiveness to issues. They shudder when they think about complaints from their users or customers. They live in fear of implementation issues that could spiral out of control, internal uprisings against the change, and cost overruns.

What They Hate

- Risky decisions: Anything that makes them look bad, costs extra money, fails to deliver results, or blows up in their face;
- Endless meetings with the internal decision team; vested interests, hidden agendas, and turf wars; squeaky wheels and Luddites; revisiting issues over and over again with no movement;
- Boring PowerPoint presentations that put them to sleep;
- Competitive badmouthing; and
- Bad numbers, inflated projections, and pie-in-the-sky promises.

Seller's Role

When working with people who suffer from Frazzled Customer Syndrome, you need to:

- Understand and influence their decision-making criteria.
- Leverage your expertise to help them make the best possible decision.
- Reduce their perception of risk.
- Differentiate yourself from competitors.

- Follow their rules, if they have them, so you don't get booted out.
- Guide them through the decision-making process.
- Limit their options, so they don't get overwhelmed.

Big Challenge

Stand out from all your competitors (both internal and external) as offering the best possible option for their business issue or opportunity. In a world of look-alike products and services, crazy-busy buyers would prefer to lump you all together in one category and use price to make their decision, rather than assessing which firm offers the best value.

Mission Accomplished

Even after your prospect says, "We want YOU!" potential show-stoppers could still derail this decision. So until you get all the details worked out, it's still not a done deal.

SNAP Considerations

Although you're close to achieving your goal, it's still important to keep the SNAP Rules in mind.

Simple

Even hot prospects cool off when they start to realize everything they need to do to make a change in their organization. To prevent this, root out any complexities. Most of all, provide strong leadership to guide your prospect through the messy decision-making process.

iNvaluable

Unless you personally bring value, you're disposable. If your prospects don't sense that you bring any worthwhile expertise to the relationship, they will go with the most cost-effective solution.

Aligned

Having a solid business case is a start, but you also need someone to care. Companies are now looking for alignment with their risk temperament: Are you safe enough? They also want to be sure that you're a good fit with their corporate culture.

Priority

Newton's Law is now working for you. Usually a body in motion tends to stay in motion. But things can get bogged down, so you have to keep the momentum moving forward. The stronger you're aligned with corporate priorities, the better.

Final Caveat

Working with prospects at this stage of their decision making is all about choices and certainty. To win their business, they must determine that:

- Your product, service, or solution is the best option for their business needs.
- Money spent on your product, service, or solution is the best use of corporate funds.
- Your company has the depth of expertise necessary to help them achieve their objectives without any glitches.

- Working with your company is the least risky decision of all their options.
- What they're paying for your offering can easily be justified, and even if it costs more, it's worth it.

These are the new challenges that you need to address in the third decision. This is when all your hard work either pays off or turns out to be a colossal waste of time. Pay attention to the new skills needed at this point in your customer's buying process; they're very different from the earlier stages.

27

Selling to Hot Prospects

inally! You're dealing with prospects who are ready to make that purchase decision. Like Pavlov's dogs, you're salivating because you know it's just a short time before you get the business.

If only it were that simple. The reality is you've just entered the next phase of your prospects' decision-making process. If you've been working with this company to get them to this point, you're in a strong position. The opportunity is yours to win, but it's also yours to lose.

Additionally, you'll be adding new third-decision prospects into your sales funnel—ones that you're just starting a relationship with. They might be:

* Referrals from your other customers or business relationships;
* People who discovered you online as they were searching for information;

- Companies you uncover during your prospecting that need to make a change now; and
- Consultants who've been hired to do all the preliminary research and present their client with the top three alternatives.

Working with prospects at this stage of their decision-making process is what all of us dream about. Now all we have to do is let them know about the incredible value of our offering, right?

Wrong! The third decision is fundamentally different from the second decision. The game has changed, and there are new rules for being a winner. You now need to transition your relationship to focus on what your prospects need from you at this point.

The Biggest Goof That Sellers Make

Your challenge now is to avoid the seduction of this low-hanging fruit. It's so powerful and so tempting to throw yourself at this opportunity: "Take me! Take me!" Okay. I'm being a bit dramatic here, but I really want to make my point. Let me give you a personal example, to show you how easy it is to get caught up in this seduction.

A few years ago, my primary business was helping large local firms shorten time to revenue on new product introductions. I'd just launched my Selling to Big Companies Web site to help small businesses gain access to my expertise.

When the phone rang, I answered absentmindedly. But when the caller announced that he was from Southwest Airlines,

I snapped to attention. He'd been all over my new Web site, was very impressed, and also very interested in my training programs. The airline was going to be putting its salespeople through training in the not-too-distant future and was evaluating its options. When I asked who else he was looking at, I was delighted to be included with the industry biggies.

Mr. Southwest had dozens of questions about my content, delivery models, remote training options, learning reinforcement, and more. I answered every single one of them in glorious detail. When he requested a proposal, I asked, "How soon?" When he answered that he wanted it in two days, I quickly agreed.

The proposal I sent to him via e-mail covered everything we had talked about in our conversation, plus a full range of pricing options. I never heard from Mr. Southwest again.

It was my own fault. I mistakenly let my own eagerness to have this marquis customer outweigh my common sense. I should have slowed things down, asked tough questions, uncovered his decision criteria, and found out about the competitors. Instead, I blindly babbled on, trying to impress him with my offering. The truth is I really needed the business at that time. After spending many months and lots of money to create SellingtoBigCompanies.com, I was running short on cash. I should have known better, but I was seduced by the opportunity.

Over and over again, I see other sellers make similar mistakes when they have a hot prospect on the line. Like me, they expound on their capabilities and benefits. They willingly provide detailed information and do tons of extra work to create proposals or presentations—anything the prospects want.

While that puts you into the "nice" seller category, it doesn't help your prospects make the best decision for their organization.

Nor does it enable you to separate yourself from your competitors. You just come across as an overeager beaver. And usually you don't get the business.

The other related problem is with the prospect who says "We're going to change" but who really means "We're seriously considering it, but haven't quite decided." While hot prospects hold the promise of big paychecks, there's still much to be done to get their business. And the first thing you need to do is find out whether your prospect is at the second or third decision stage so you know how to work with them.

When You're Late to the Party

Before you get caught up in the seduction of the low-hanging fruit, slow down, catch your breath and gather your wits about you. Just because you have an interested prospect does not mean that a sale is imminent. In fact, depending on your product or service, it may be months before you have a signed contract.

Even more important, so much has already gone on in the organization to get them to this point, and you're in catch-up mode. You need to figure out, as soon as humanly possible, why this hot prospect decided to call your company.

Rather than jumping on the opportunity, first perform your due diligence. Go online and research the firm. See if you can surmise the issues they are facing, the motivation behind their call, or what their status quo might be. Also, think about current customers you have who are in similar businesses and what you know about their needs. The smarter you are when you have a conversation, the better.

Even if your prospect catches you on the phone, buy yourself some time to get grounded in their organization before you talk. After you get a sense of their situation, you might say, "Thanks for calling, Eric. I think we can help you with this. But I'm running to a meeting right now. Can we set aside twenty minutes tomorrow morning to continue this conversation?" They will invariably agree. So now you have time to do your research.

At this stage of your customer's decision-making process, *how* you sell is more important than *what* you sell.

If prospects grant you time, they've determined that you've crossed the "acceptable" threshold. These educated customers nearly always check out your Web site prior to meeting with you. They have a fairly decent understanding of your offering. You may not have the best product or service, but it's okay enough. Your price may not be the lowest price, but it's probably in the right range.

But if you want to win the business, being "acceptable" is a setup for failure. You need to be invaluable to decision makers, helping them improve their business. And you need to help them make their complicated decision.

Revisiting the Mind Meld

Recently I did a workshop with a technology company that wanted to shorten its eighteen-month sales cycle. The people at the session were from Sales, Tech Support, Marketing, and Presales. We started by discussing the primary challenges hampering their ability to close the business and what they'd already tried that was effective and ineffective.

Then I changed the direction, because we weren't getting at the bigger issue. First, we created a prototypical account and identified all the people in the company usually involved in the decision-making process. Then we assigned a person to "be" each of these individuals. As best as we could, we tried to match their expertise.

With the mind meld in place, I posed the pivotal question: "How do you make decisions for these kinds of products in your company?" The role-players had to speak "as if" they were the decision maker.

For the next two hours, we mapped out their decision process from start to finish. We included all the teams that got involved at the various points (e.g., Marketing, IT, Customer Support, Tech Services, Finance), what they had to do, and how long that took. By the time we finished detailing the entire process, the flip charts covered an entire wall—and sure enough, it took at least eighteen months to get an agreement.

Additionally, our role-playing decision makers clashed at various times over differing priorities, expectations, issues, assumptions, and agendas. Even in a simulation, it wasn't pretty.

As we stepped back to review the exercise from a sales perspective, we had a whole new take on what was required to keep things moving along. It became glaringly obvious that it would be impossible to shorten the sales cycle doing what they'd always done.

The process itself was draining the lifeblood from the decision, making it a burden that was difficult to champion—especially in tough times. Overwhelmed decision makers got bogged down in the process as they did their best to figure out what to do next. It was complicated and messy. People who initially championed the project lost their oomph for it because the process was moving at a snail's pace.

Several things became readily apparent. First of all, the

sellers needed to lead instead of pushing their solution or wait-ing for the next customer directive. The solution was just too complex for their prospects to figure out on their own. Addition-ally, because of the complexity, the business case got lost in the process. We realized just how much the salespeople needed to keep it at the forefront of the discussion. It was "why" they were going through this extensive process—and it was very valuable to their company. Finally, risk emerged as the primary decision inhibitor. The sellers' failure to deal with it head-on was slowing things way down. Clearly better sales tools were needed to help their prospects feel more secure about moving ahead.

At this point, these revelations shouldn't be a surprise, since we addressed them in earlier chapters. But how they play out in the third decision is different.

Get Your Ducks in a Row

To be successful at this stage, you should go through these exer-cises with your typical customer's decision-making process. You've already identified the primary decision makers and com-pleted a Buyer's Matrix on each one. You've created a customer persona for each of these positions, too. Now it's time to:

Create a Decision Map.

Walk through the decision from their perspective—not yours. Map it out, detailing every likely step in their journey to closure. Add in the time frames. Identify the angst they feel.

When you're done, the real work begins. Ask yourself and/or your colleagues: How can we make it easier? How can we ensure a strong business case? What tools do we need? What can I personally do to become the differentiator?

Knowing this information is invaluable to you in planning your strategy. Post the map you've created so it's visible as a constant reminder of how your prospect decides. Keep thinking about the questions. The more you ask them, the more answers you'll get.

Landscape the Competition.

Once you've created a map, you need to factor in the competition, since it's highly likely they'll be vying for this same opportunity. Identify the primary competitors you'll encounter and do your research on them. If you have colleagues, share your competitive knowledge.

What do you know about their products or services? What are their strengths and weaknesses? What strategies are they using in their sales? What are prospects, customers, and analysts saying about them?

This street-fresh information is invaluable. Share it openly and share it often. Then start comparing yourself to your prime competitors. Where are your real advantages? What value do they bring? What's your weakest link? How can you minimize it?

In the remainder of this section, we'll look at the application of the SNAP Rules to the third decision. While many books have been written on presentations, proposals, beating competition, and more, our emphasis will continue to be on simplicity, alignment, personal value, and maintaining momentum.

28

Simple: Make the Decision as Easy as Possible

You know you have a better shot at wooing your customers if you keep things simple for them, but when was the last time you really, really took this to heart and made changes in what you did?

Recently, I spoke to a group of college students majoring in sales. Jessica, who worked for a tech company as a sales intern, told of how shocked she was when she saw a proposal prepared by one of the salespeople. It was one hundred pages long, filled with corporate boilerplate covering everything that a decision maker might ever want to know—in excruciating detail. When she raised questions about it, she was told by the sales pros, "That's what we always do!" I told her that their failure to change would hurt their chances of winning, and could even get them tossed out of the decision-making process prematurely.

As architect and Zen gardener Dr. Koichi Kawana says, "Simplicity means the achievement of maximum effect with minimal means." When you examine everything you do through that lens, it shifts what you do and how you do it.

Assume the Role of Decision Guide

In addition to their already overwhelming workload, your frazzled prospects have to go through multiple steps internally to get the go-ahead to change. Along the way, they have to deal with innumerable issues and challenges. In many cases, they're suffering from severe decision naïveté because it's been ages since they made a change. Or they're "first timers" who've never made these types of decisions before. The odds are certainly stacked against you.

One of the best ways you can have "maximum effect with minimal means" is to take on the leadership role at this stage in the decision-making process. You've helped other companies make these decisions. You know what they struggled with. You know the issues they ran into. You've walked this path before.

You are in the perfect position to become your prospects' guide—someone who helps them get to their desired destination. Your expertise can really help them. But remember, when you're a guide, you can't be pushy with your own agenda. You can't start "selling" your stuff. Instead, you must remain consultative and helpful—which will really differentiate you from your competitors and speed up the decision-making process.

It's hard to let go of your urge to sell, especially when you've put it off for so long. But trust me, you'll have a chance to do that when your prospects are ready to evaluate their options knowledgeably, with the right people involved.

Be Matter-of-Fact

As a decision guide, you'll need to have matter-of-fact discussions with your prospects about all sorts of things, which may at first seem a bit bold to you. Initially you may even feel as if you're overstepping your bounds. But having frank conversations will help your prospects make the smoothest, most painless, and fastest decision.

There are different ways to approach the third decision, depending on how long you've been working with your prospects.

For nurtured prospects. If you've helped companies with the second decision, to initiate change, you're likely already acting as a guide. To keep yourself in that position for the third decision, you might say:

Now that you've made the decision to change, let's start working on doing what it takes to get the official approval. I've worked with dozens of companies on this. Let me ask you a few questions so we'll know how to get this to happen with as much ease as possible.

For new prospects. If you've just uncovered them through your prospecting efforts or they've contacted your company, you need to set the stage for being the decision guide by saying:

It sounds like you're ready to make a change in the not-too-distant future. I've worked with a number of other companies who have been through this, so if you don't mind, I'd like to ask you a few questions to determine the best way to proceed.

By making these statements confidently, you're typically granted the leadership role. However, your ability to ask thoughtful, relevant, and provocative questions is the key to your success.

Whatever you do, you do *not* want to be in a responder position, simply answering your prospects' questions. Why not? Because prospects typically focus on details such as price, features, and capabilities. The differences between you and your competitors is often minute, and you can easily lose an opportunity over an insignificant trifle.

Instead, you need to get your prospects to see and experience the total value that you and your company can bring. That's why it's essential to be the leader.

Leading with Questions

A good guide needs accurate information on a variety of topics (see the questions that follow). You'll want to ask most, if not all, of these questions over the course of the decision-making process. You don't need to cram them into a single meeting.

Driving Force

Use these questions at the outset to help you determine where your prospects are in the decision-making process and their impetus for change:

Help me understand the business drivers behind this desire to change. What are you hoping to accomplish?

Have you already received the go-ahead to make the change or are you still investigating?

Why are you suddenly unhappy with status quo? Has your company established new objectives or are you experiencing problems?

Whom are you currently using? Why wouldn't you keep using them?

Why did you decide to contact our company? At this stage in your research, what is of most interest to you?

Decision Process

Use these questions to get a good sense of your prospect's understanding of their decision-making process. Also, listen for what they are unable to answer, to learn in which areas you could provide guidance.

What's kept you from making a change before now?

What's your process for making this decision?

Why wouldn't you use your own internal team to handle this?

Why would you want to change from your current vendor—especially since it can be so disruptive?

What are your timelines? When would you like to have this solution up and running?

Who needs to get involved? Who else?

Usually when we work on decisions like this, [department name] is always part of the process. Where do they stand on this?

What do you need from me in order to get final approval?

Risk/Concern

While you may dislike talking about risks and concerns, the failure to bring them up can create significant problems for you. Use these questions to get any showstoppers out on the table:

What are the drawbacks for making a change?

Based on my experience, decisions like this typically entail issues such as competing priorities or different perspectives. (Note: Review your decision map from the previous chapter and raise the appropriate concerns.)

How have you handled this to date?

What are you anticipating coming up?

How about the politics involved?

Since there are always people against these change initiatives, where do you expect the greatest resistance to come from?

What happens if you don't change? What are the consequences?

Evaluation Criteria Questions

Use these questions to get an understanding of how your prospects will be assessing competitors and to what extent they know how to make these kinds of decisions:

Who else are you looking at?

What criteria do you plan on using to make your decision?

What's important to you in the firm/person you select to do business with?

How will you differentiate between the various options?

How will you measure success?

As Sharon Drew Morgen, author of *Dirty Little Secrets*, says, "Until buyers understand and know how to mitigate the risks that a new solution brings to their culture, they will do nothing." In other words, you need to make them see how you can make life simpler for them. That's why your ability to "lead with questions" is essential to your success.

At Performance Marketing Group, sellers are always prepared to talk with information-seeking prospects. They've developed their own set of predefined questions so that, as CEO Ed Hennessy says, "when a savvy, sophisticated potential customer contacts their firm they know the steps to guide them, and how to make their buying decision simple and straightforward." They also do this to ensure that their reps don't give prospects any possible justification for seeking out another source.

To make sure you're ready for the prospect who calls you,

prepare a list of ten questions you can use at this stage of the sales process. Keep them by your phone and pull them out when needed.

Bring Up Tough Stuff and Missing Matters

If your prospects struggle to answer any of your questions, you've uncovered a real opportunity to help them with the decision-making process. For example, let's say that the VP of Sales has contacted a training company looking for ways to help increase sales. As you read these three mini-dialogues, think about how you'd feel if you were the prospect.

> SELLER: You mentioned that several of your regional managers think your salespeople just need to close harder and more often.
>
> PROSPECT: That's true. But I think we need to improve other skills as well.
>
> SELLER: In working with other clients, typically their closing problems are a symptom of a deeper problem. Focusing on closing harder and more often just exacerbates the issue. Unless your regional managers understand this, what we recommend won't work. Let's set up a conference call with them to talk about it.

> SELLER: Based on my experience, technology is a real factor these days in shortening the sales cycle. What Sales 2.0 tools do your salespeople use on a regular basis?
>
> PROSPECT: We have a CRM system, but that's about it. They're not a very tech-savvy group.
>
> SELLER: That's a start, but if you really want to move decisions along faster, that's something we'll need to address right

away. Are you open to looking at increasing your capabilities in this area?

SELLER: How will you be evaluating the various companies you're looking at?

PROSPECT: We wanted a company with experience in our industry, strong references, and one we felt would resonate best with our reps.

SELLER: That's a good start. We often find that people who don't often make decisions in this area will overlook key factors that can have a major impact on their ability to achieve successful outcomes. We have some materials that may give you some fresh insights. Would you be interested in seeing them?

As you read these dialogues, did you notice how potential showstoppers, related issues, and decision criteria were easily integrated in the conversation? These are important matters that need to be discussed. Most of us hate to bring up issues that could get in the way of our getting the business. But once you bring them out into the open, they're just facts that need to be dealt with.

More important, you're helping prospective customers identify and confront the quagmires ahead, under the guidance of an expert who's worked with other companies facing the same problems and issues.

More "Keep It Simple" Strategies

Here are several more strategies you can use to simplify decisions for your prospects:

Create a Road Map.

Once prospects enter the third decision, they want to work with people who have a logical and sequential approach to achieving their desired outcome. That's why it's so helpful to be able to show them a plan for how you'll work together.

Executive recruiter Rebecca Patt uses her 8-Step Success Process to differentiate herself from competitors. She says, "They pay me to execute a proven process to identify an ideal candidate. I send it to them in writing too. They feel more confident about the value they get knowing what they can expect me to do."

Inside sales expert Trish Bertuzzi, CEO of the Bridge Group, adds, "Once you've done a good job of laying the foundation and you feel you're a serious contender for the business, be assumptive in your conversations. Say, 'When we move forward, we'll have this accomplished by xxx.' Have them visualize a calendar with you that includes milestones of deliverables and results."

Stress What Stays the Same.

Anytime people have to change, it's disconcerting. Tom Searcy, author of *RFPs Suck!*, suggests that you make sure the customer clearly understands which of its many systems will not change as a consequence of their doing a deal with you. He says, "the more you can reassure the buyers that changes will be minimal, the higher your chances of success will be."

When I work with clients, I always make sure they know that Selling to Big Companies workshops complement their existing training investment rather than replace it. This always elicits an audible sigh of relief.

What's the point of all this? With frazzled customers, the easier you can make things, the more successful you'll be. Complexity kills sales and sends you spiraling into the dreaded D-Zone, where hot opportunities gradually cool off and then disappear forever.

Be rigorous in analyzing your sales approach, sales tools, and company policies for complexity. Always ask, "How can we make it simpler? How can we be easier to do business with?" Complexity is simply an obstacle that needs to be removed.

29

Aligned: Balancing the Value-Risk Equation

I n a business-to-business environment, it's tempting to think that it's all about the numbers: If the ROI or payback is good, the decision to change from the status quo is a "no-brainer." And if your proposal offers the best pricing, then you're bound to win the deal.

But that simplistic view just doesn't hold true in real life—even with today's frazzled customers, who'd love to base their decisions on simple arithmetic alone. Instead, they're left with a complex balancing act, trying to determine if the value of making the change outweighs the cost of staying the same. They factor in everything that could possibly go wrong and then, finally, they make their selection as the logical choice emerges.

Then why do so many people make such stupid decisions? One of my former clients, a 1980s rock-star high-tech firm, met their demise because the CEO kept coming up with brilliant (but unworkable) schemes to save the company when the market changed.

Another client invested millions setting up an entirely new division to sell solutions, not products. But they really didn't have any. Nor did they want to hire the necessary expertise till after the salespeople won the projects—which, of course, they never could, because it was all smoke and mirrors.

And how many companies have implemented expensive CRM systems, trained their entire sales force, and then watched things fail miserably. Clearly, there's more to making a decision to change than we initially anticipated.

Be Compelling

People make decisions because what happens in their company matters to them. Believing that they're dealing with a credible firm that's proposed a sound concept is the starting point. But, as Chip and Dan Heath point out in *Made to Stick*, "For people to take action, they have to care."

Company executives care when you show them ideas on how to:

- Achieve their desired future or growth initiatives;
- Create first-mover or sustainable competitive advantage;
- Turn around failing businesses or stop the bleeding; and
- Maintain their current business more elegantly or with fewer resources.

They need a vision from you regarding what's possible—really possible, given where they are today. Maurice Janssen Duijghuij-sen, sales director at an IT services company, understands that.

When he met with a potential client, he used just one slide that graphically depicted the prospect's present situation and a year 2020 vision. In that future state, he showed what value his company could add.

The result? A double-digit million-euro deal. Plus, later that year he attended a seminar where his client spoke and saw him using the same slide. Maurice says, "I helped [him] dream and see the future as he wanted it to be."

For many of your customers, that "caring" comes about because they see a better way. They may be struggling to reach their objectives in the time frames expected and with the available resources. They've spent lots of time researching the issue and looking at options. They "know" it will make a difference, and they can see your product or service working in their business environment.

Getting conceptual buy-in with someone who cares is not just about numbers. It's about compelling stories—told verbally, in written format, and in presentations with simple graphics that pull people into what's possible.

"Deliver a killer presentation that tells the story of how their lives will be better when they use your solution," advises enterprise account manager Justyn Howard. "Back it up with stats and similar client examples. Make sure you eliminate what's unnecessary; get rid of bullets and get rid of words. Use images to relay your ideas. Your slides should quickly encapsulate the main idea, but the audience should be listening to you."

That's what it takes to engage people and get their conceptual buy-in. Get them excited. Remove the drudge and toil factors. When you can do that, they care—and you really need that if you're going to do business with their organization. Otherwise, it's all a moot exercise in financial justification.

Clarify the Business Value

Usually it's the business case that opens the door for you and creates the conversation. And it's the business case that seals the deal. But in my work with a variety of organizations, I've found there are several very different ways they look at this.

Financially Driven Decisions

These companies truly pay attention to how their corporate funding is spent—especially if the decision involves lots of money or the offering is perceived as a commodity. This may include software, business services, capital equipment, and travel. The company may also be in financial distress.

When supply chain or purchasing gets involved, then you know it's all about the money. In many cases, they've eliminated the easy savings. If you can show them how to do more with less, they'll be interested. They want to see the hard numbers, too.

"It Makes Sense" Decisions

Many buyers don't require an airtight business case before they choose to move ahead. They know that what they're doing isn't working great. They know that their goals will be unattainable unless they move off the status quo. In short, what you've proposed makes good sense to them. They may, however, need you to work with them to create a financial business case required by their boss or CFO.

One of the most overlooked but powerful ways of getting numbers you can use is to ask your prospects about their perception of the value. Simple questions like this are extremely effective:

- If you could eliminate this problem, what difference would it make to your organization?
- If you were able to achieve this objective, how will this help you [typical areas of value creation]?
- How else would it help? What other business value would it provide?

Sometimes prospects need just a bit more help to move beyond the myopic view of the financial investment. Sales optimization expert Shiera O'Brien suggests presenting the "multiplier effect" to demonstrate the longer-term value of your offering. "Even though a prospect may spend $5,000 to get even a small improvement today (e.g., 5 percent), it can lead to significant profit improvement over time," she says. "To reinforce this, design a 'multiplier calculator.' It gets prospects away from the 'spend today' and moves them to the real returns over time of that 5 percent improvement."

Cost of Inaction

Finally, you need to work with your prospects to determine the costs of doing nothing. In many cases, they're trying to determine if the transition to a new vendor or bringing in an outside resource is worth the effort. Ask them the following questions:

- How will staying with the status quo impact your business?
- What about the cost of the continued problems?

- What won't you be able to achieve? What does that mean to you from a business perspective?

Management consultant Bob Apollo advises sellers to be wary of prospects who can't easily articulate the consequences of inaction. In short, "they run the risk of doing all the hard work to eliminate competitors and get themselves chosen, but then never getting bought."

Unless you can help them quantify the costs of doing nothing, they won't necessarily know. In fact, staying with the status quo can be a "you bet your business" decision—one where they fall progressively farther behind because they failed to take the necessary actions.

Are You Risky Business?

Years ago, I was meeting with the VP of Sales for a hot telecom company. They'd loved my proposal, so I figured we were getting together to kick off the project.

"I'm afraid I have bad news for you," the VP said. "We think your training program is superior to the other ones we've looked at. Your pricing is fair. And your ability to tie it in with our new product launch is unsurpassed. However, we've decided to go with your competitor."

My jaw dropped. I stared at him in shock. Then he continued, "If you get hit by a Mack truck, our entire training investment is gonzo. We just can't do that." In short, he meant that my company was too small to do business with. Working with me entailed more risk than he was willing to take.

That was the day when the concept of "risk" truly hit home

for me. Our prospects deal with it all the time. But often we, as sellers, are totally blind to what a risky decision we can be.

In today's business environment, we have to be aligned not only with our prospects' business objectives but also their risk temperament. To your prospects, risk means the cost of making a mistake. It could be financial, social, psychological, or even emotional. Risk is about fear of change.

Chris Mercer, CEO of Mercer Appraisal, found this out early in the life of his company: "When we were smaller, we realized that there's a concept called 'safety' in the minds of most buyers. From their perspective, it's a multi-variable function of size, longevity, customer list, perceived quality, external affirmations (speeches, articles, books), and many other things. We've been working for more than twenty-five years to be the safe choice in our field."

That's what we all need to do. But it all starts with identifying what your prospects perceive as risky. Here is a list of just a few things they could fret over:

- Projects not delivering results;
- Losing money; missed deadlines;
- Your company's financial solvency;
- Cultural fit; compatibility;
- Quality of your work;
- If your expertise is right for them;
- Accuracy of claims;
- Your length of time in business;
- If you're too big to care about their business; and
- If you're too small to handle their account.

You may pooh-pooh some of these as no big deals, but believe me, I never thought a Mack truck would impact my ability to get business, either.

Minimize the Risk

Nobody wants to make a bad decision. People don't like the unknown; they fear it. They're leery about making any change when there's the possibility of a career-derailing failure.

As discussed earlier, when you take on the role of a sales guide, your prospects immediately feel like they're in good hands. Here are some more strategies that can reduce your prospects' perceived risk in doing business with you or your company:

Leverage qualitative data.

The more data you have that supports your proposal, the better. Internal documentation (case studies, assessments) should be combined with external sources of validation. If at all possible, share relevant analyst's reports, studies, and articles.

Ensure transparency.

Today's prospects want to know the truth, so don't shade it. In this social media age, where customers freely voice their opinions online, you can be assured that any issue about your offering, customer service, and financial stability can easily be uncovered.

Manage their expectations.

Marketing strategist Kristine Maveus-Evenson says, "If both of you are clear about objectives, milestones, budget, scope of work, deliverables, and timelines, this builds trust. If you discuss this from the onset, it eliminates the FUD [fear, uncertainty, and doubt], which helps to mitigate their perception of risk."

Engage multiple stakeholders.

Prior to any proposal or presentation, talk with all the people involved. Consultant Jeff Garrison recommends talking to them for at least fifteen minutes to get their perspectives. This reduces the risk that your primary contact will be blindsided by turf issues or hidden agendas at the end of the decision-making process.

Offer references.

Your willingness to openly share references with prospects makes a big difference. Certainly, you have your top customers who love you. But also consider offering your three newest customers, because they're most likely to relate to your prospects' fears. Because they've just chosen you, they're likely to be strong advocates.

When your prospects are making the third decision, certainty is a crucial factor. Unless they feel confident they're making a solid business decision, one that will help them achieve their business objectives, they'll stay with what they have. It's just plain easier—and certainly less scary.

If you ignore your prospects' fears, they won't go away. Instead, they'll lurk silently under the surface, wreaking havoc with their nerves, until your prospects finally decide that changing now isn't best for them—even if it is.

30

iNvaluable: Be the One They Want to Work With

If you've made it this far in your prospects' decision-making process, your competence is now assumed. They consider your product or service to be "good enough" to meet their needs. However, when they see minimal differentiation between you and your competitor, tough times loom. You need to do something to be the preferred choice.

Which reminds me of the existential question: "What happens when the irresistible force meets the unmovable object?"

After years of puzzling over this question, I now know that the irresistible force nearly always wins. Unlike corporations, decision makers are human beings who have strong feelings about what they're doing. They're highly influenced by your competence, candor, and commitment to their success—even though they may not be able to clearly articulate this.

When I worked as a sales manager at Xerox, we regularly surveyed customers to identify the most influential criteria in their decision making. My average reps' customers bought the Xerox brand; it was safe. My top sellers' customers chose them! Because they focused on needs, brought value, and established a trusted-adviser relationship, top sellers invariably won the business—even when their products cost 25 percent more, had fewer capabilities, and weren't as good.

That's the irresistible force in action. Every seller can become an invaluable asset if they choose to be. This is a choice you need to personally make. While it requires you to learn, study, research, think, and lead, it also pays huge dividends. The average seller can't compete with you—especially when you're dealing with a frazzled customer who really needs all the value you bring. In short, the time you invest here makes selling exponentially easier.

Caroline Kirby, former top car seller and now technology rep, says, "I don't care what you're selling. People are in fear. Your job is to establish trust—which you do by being authentic, caring about your customers, engendering feelings of subject matter expertise, and making the selection easy and pain-free." Amen to that!

Let's take a look at some strategies you can use to differentiate yourself from competitors and win business with crazy-busy buyers.

Collaborate "As If" They're a Customer

"Is this a person (company) I want to work with on a long-term basis?" That's what your prospects are thinking—all the time. To be most effective, drop the "sales" mentality and start working with your prospects as if they've already hired you. This shifts your relationship to a new level from the get-go.

Several years ago a regional engineering firm contacted me

about helping with an upcoming presentation. I worked with the lead engineer and business developer to develop an entire strategy based on this concept. We knew that the other RFP respondents would likely spend their one hour talking about their firm, their specialties, the qualifications of the team they'd assembled, and their prestigious client base. Instead of doing that, my client (who was competing against the giants for the first time) put together a handout covering these items.

At the beginning of the meeting, my client's primary presenter said, "All the information you requested about our company is in this handout. We'll gladly answer any questions you might have about it. But what we'd really like to do today is focus more on your challenge and what it's going to take to resolve it. We have some questions that we believe may have an impact on achieving your desired outcome."

With that opening, he caught their undivided attention. The first slides focused on their current situation. My client asked preplanned questions on vital topics to verify his understanding of the status quo and learn more in-depth information. These simple-to-answer questions were designed to get the prospects talking.

After that, my client brought up several key issues they'd uncovered in reviewing the RFP. This led to a discussion on root causes versus presenting symptoms. My client then offered new ways to tackle the problem that were less disruptive. Then they challenged the prospects' thinking on some "must have" criteria, suggesting options they thought might work better. This stirred up another highly engaging conversation.

In short, they started working on this $400,000-plus project during their presentation. The results? Because it was their first time competing against the giants, my client hoped to make it into the final three. This in itself was a big win!

But the result was even more surprising. Instead of going to a second round of more intensive presentations with the finalists, my client was awarded the contract on the spot. Everyone on the committee wanted to work with them.

Many people are afraid of giving away their ideas before a contract is signed, but often that's the best way to win the business. Here's another example.

Recently Anne Miller, author of *Metaphorically Selling*, was competing for a training project. The COO couldn't decide; he just wanted to "feel" that the person would add value. Anne showed him what she'd done for other customers. She raised questions about pre-work, which he hadn't considered. She shared strategies to help the reps better retain the information. Ultimately, she was chosen.

What would you do for a customer that you'd never think about doing for a prospect? Are you holding back something because you're afraid they'll steal it? Are you approaching your meetings as a chance to really "strut your stuff" or are you getting to work?

For many sellers, this is a new concept. Think about how you can be more collegial—even before you start working together. It's worth it.

Make Differentiation Easier

Early on in my Xerox sales career, I had a couple of tough competitors who were hard to beat. One sold a copier that had an automatic On/Off switch. Customers loved this energy-saving feature, feeling that it would help them reduce costs. Another competitor's product was 25 percent cheaper and had better copy quality.

Because I hated losing to these vendors when I believed that my company was best, I threw myself into understanding them at a deeper level. I learned that the big energy savings was really the equivalent of having a light bulb on all the time. From that, I calculated the true savings. The other competitor used different drum technology, which significantly shortened its machines' life span. This meant copy quality varied frequently and the total cost of ownership was much higher.

Because potential buyers didn't know how to make an accurate comparison, I decided to educate them on what to look for. To do this, I created a competitive checklist my prospects could use in their conversations with all vendors. I included their typical comparative items, then added new ones of my own.

CRITERIA	MY COMPANY	VENDOR B	VENDOR C
Speed			
Paper size			
Reduction capabilities			
Drum type			
Annual supply cost			
Total cost of ownership			
Like-for-like replacement			

When I presented this checklist to them, I went through each item and filled in Xerox's information. When I got to the more complex ones, I gave a thorough explanation of the differences in technologies, the overall total cost of ownership, and the risk factors involved.

Doing this fundamentally shifted the dynamic of the meeting, and my success rate. My competitors were pushing their products. I was the expert helping them make a sound decision. That's the position you want to be in!

Sales effectiveness consultant Christian Maurer stresses the importance of competitive research so you can ascertain which strong points the competitors will be emphasizing. With this knowledge in hand, he suggests talking to your prospects about which points they care about most. According to him, "Not only does this clarify where you can differentiate, but you add value simply by helping them get this clarity."

Act as the Trusted Resource

Whenever your prospects consider the differences between you and your competitors to be minimal, it's up to you to change that perception by proactively being the go-to resource. Here are some more examples of how to differentiate your products or services:

Comparing Apples to Oranges

Recently I showed a large business services firm how to use this approach to take business away from firmly entrenched competitors. In my training program with them, they kept saying, "Their prices are cheaper, but it's not an apples-to-oranges comparison. Customers pay more in the long run because of all the extra charges that aren't included."

As a group, we brainstormed the numerous services that were excluded from the competitor's quote. Then we talked about how to educate customers with this strategy. The result? They were given the opportunity to review the previous year's billings to do an accurate comparison—which ultimately yielded an increased win rate on bids with their price-sensitive customers.

Dealing with Super Savvy Customers

Technology sales pro Kate Reschenberg frequently deals with prospects who've done a lot of research prior to contacting her firm. They know what they want and start peppering her with questions. Rather than simply responding, or "selling" her offering, she operates as if it's simply her job to make sure they get the right product.

Her questions set her apart. She asks, "Have you thought of . . . ?" "What are you doing to solve . . . ?" By raising these questions, her prospects realize her depth of knowledge in the field. Not only does this separate her from her colleagues, but it also makes her well-researched prospects realize they may not have thought of everything. The result? They begin to see her as a trusted adviser.

Bringing News They Can Use

Any time you do this, you set yourself apart from competitors.

When consultant Babette Burdick's prospects mull over whether they should go ahead or not, she brings them up-to-date information on industry trends to further support their decision and solidify her position.

Intellectual property isn't just the domain of big companies anymore. When you bring your expertise to your customers, it is a powerful differentiator that trumps most other choice points.

Truth and Consequences

While we're all taught to be truthful when we're growing up, sometimes it can be really hard to speak up—especially when it might mean losing the business. But there is nothing that endears you to a prospect more than putting your own pocketbook on the line.

Several years back, the new VP of Sales and Marketing from my biggest client hired me to design the entire launch plan for a high-profile new product. To make a long story short, I gradually became aware he was using the plan to look good but had no intention of doing what it took to make it a success. I resigned from the project—even though it hurt me financially.

A few months later, I received a call from my former client's new general manager. The VP had been sent packing and she wanted to know about the status of the launch project. When I told her about quitting, she promptly hired me to finish it. Why? Because I was someone who talked straight with her.

Being truthful really does matter. Here are several other examples of the difference it can make.

As director of business development for a marketing agency, Kent Speakman knows that candor has a huge impact on his sales success. In one situation, he was the only competitor bidding on a big request for proposal (RFP) who pointed out the flaws in the original concept and presented an alternative strategy. He won the business.

With another prospect who wanted proposals for a major rebranding initiative, Kent submitted a solid proposal that turned out to be the highest priced. Because he'd built trust in the process of working with the prospect, they called him to figure out how to make it work. Together they reviewed competitors' proposals, marketing budgets, and more. Ultimately he came up with a creative proposal that enabled him to land the client.

When Laurie Weed was working as a major account rep for a copier company, it was always tough to dislodge a long-term incumbent. That's why she was delighted when she received an opportunity to bid on a portion of business at a big company. Shortly after she submitted the proposal, she received a call from her competitor (the incumbent) who wanted to interview her for a position. At the end of the conversation, he said, "By the way, the big company has decided to stay with us."

Devastated, she wrote a gracious note to her prospect, thanking her for the opportunity and hoping they could work together in the future. Several days later, her prospect called, wondering why she'd received the letter. Laurie shared the story—and was promptly awarded the contract that afternoon.

Your prospects like truth-tellers. Don't be afraid to speak up. But make sure they understand the context of what you're sharing. You care. You want them to succeed. That's why you're talking.

Decisions today are rarely about price only—even though that may be what you hear most of the time. Crazy-busy customers willingly pay more to work with sellers who make their jobs easier, help them sort through the clutter, and bring them useful ideas and information. You are truly the differentiator with these frazzled people. It's important that you understand this, because it's the one factor that you alone totally control.

31

Priority:
Getting the Business

The end is finally in sight. Sometimes it seems that things move painfully slow the closer you get to a done deal. The worst is when other things pop up in your customers' organization that usurp their time and steal your mindshare. That's why it's important for you to keep the momentum moving forward.

Even this far into your prospects' decision-making process, it's imperative for you to ensure they have the information they need to make their final selections. They're scared. They're risk-averse. They don't want to do anything stupid.

They've heard you talk about how good your stuff is, but you're in sales, so you're expected to strut your stuff. Now they need outside validation. If you haven't done this already, this is a good time to for you to:

- Arrange conversations with existing customers.
- Showcase video testimonials of satisfied, similar customers.

- Highlight complimentary analyst's reports or articles.
- Set up site visits to other users' facilities or your own corporate offices.

In wrapping up the third decision, I'd like to focus on presentations and proposals. Since whole books have been written on these very important topics, I recognize that I'm not doing them justice with such a small space. However, I want to share a few thoughts relevant to the SNAP Factors and working with crazy-busy decision makers.

Create SNAP-py Presentations

Many companies, in the final stages of their decision-making process, invite the finalists to give a presentation to their buying team. This is an opportunity for you to shine—or to lose the business.

If you've been asked to give a presentation, but have little history with the organization, make sure you perform your due diligence first. Find out what's important to your prospect and what they want to get out of the meeting. Review your presentation with your key contact prior to the big day to ensure you're spot-on. If not, make any necessary adjustments.

Long, boring PowerPoint presentations are absolute killers in today's business environment. But when they're combined with a seller who reads the bullet points, that's a sure setup for a presentation of mass destruction. You don't want that to happen.

It's imperative that the SNAP Factors be your guiding light in determining what information to include in your presentation and in how it's presented. To ensure success in these critical meetings, follow these steps:

1. Decide on Content

This is the story you want to tell. To start with, grab their attention by focusing on what's most important to them: their business issues and concerns, and the value they'll get from making the change.

- **Aligned:** Ensure that all content is ruthlessly relevant to your prospect.
- **Priority:** Make sure you highlight why it's important to change now.
- **Simple:** Eliminate or minimize any complexity, making change easy.

2. Develop the Slides

In the actual presentation, you tell the story and your slides simply support it. As much as possible, find photos and graphics to make your main points. To best imagine what I'm talking about, think of a children's picture book.

Each slide should be the launching pad for a key point you want to make. The fewer (seven to ten) you have, the better. Use handouts for detailed information. This forces you to prepare a conversation, not read a bunch of PowerPoint items. The results? You connect with your prospects on a whole new level.

Another emerging presentation format from Japan is called Pecha Kucha. Using this format, you present twenty images for just twenty seconds each. All told, you have six minutes and forty seconds. This forces you to concentrate on only the most relevant information and weave it together into a story. Your prospects will never get bored. Then, when it's done, you can have a conversation.

3. Build in Engagement

When your prospect is evaluating their options, you need to recognize that the content itself is only a small portion of how you're being evaluated. This is especially true when there isn't a whole lot of difference between you and your competitors.

Your prospects are deciding which company they'd feel best working with in the upcoming months and years. That's why it's imperative to think about the questions you will use to engage your prospects in a discussion. This is also where you personally can demonstrate your expertise, commitment, and caring. In short, it's how you personally become invaluable during a presentation.

If you persist in having multiple slides that fill up virtually the whole meeting, you are not differentiating yourself enough to ensure you get chosen. Your prospects want to work with people they feel comfortable with, not slide readers.

Don't just grab the PowerPoint slides that Marketing prepared for you. Invariably, they're simply product or service overviews, filled with all sorts of self-promoting puffery, technical tripe, or creative crap.

If you've been given the opportunity to present to a group of people, use it wisely. Create a SNAP-py presentation that covers the important content, tells the story of why they should work with you, and most important, ensures they get a real sense of what it's like to work collaboratively with you.

Since your presentations may involve others from your company, make sure to prep your corporate wonks ahead of time. Don't let them go into the meeting cold. Give them background about your customers' needs, issues, and concerns. Explain to them what needs to be stressed—and what needs to be avoided. If you don't, you may be sorry! (That's the voice of experience talking.)

Whatever you do, don't abdicate your responsibility for ensuring the optimal result.

Powerful and Persuasive Proposals

When buyer-turned-salesman Emilio Pedral used to review proposals submitted by potential vendors, he didn't have a lot of time to analyze the options they presented him with. "I really appreciated when the information was presented in a clear and simple way," he says. "I always checked the accuracy of the data. If it was untrue or if the offering demanded too much time to evaluate, we'd go to the next option."

As you can see, the SNAP Factors are important in proposals, too. I recently spoke at a conference with Tom Sant, author of *Persuasive Business Proposals*. He really caught my attention when he said that sellers could increase their proposal win rate by 27 percent simply by reordering the proposal into the way the customer's brain was hardwired to think. His advice? Follow your NOSE for persuasive proposals: Needs, Outcomes, Solutions, and Evidence.

When he outlined his structure, I was glad to discover it was basically identical to what I'd always recommended:

Cover Page: Replace "A Proposal for XYZ Company" with your value proposition: "Shrinking Time to Revenue on New Product Launches."

Executive Summary: Since these one to two pages are the most read part of your proposal, make sure to invest time in making them super snappy. Highlight your prospect's desired outcomes, give a basic overview of your proposed solution, and explain why you're the best choice and what they can expect from their investment.

Business Case: Align their objectives, key issues, and challenges, and their impact on their business. Make sure the key points pop up, via bullet points and callout boxes. Whenever possible, use graphics, because they simplify difficult concepts. Real-world examples (e.g., "You'll save more money than the value of five BMWs") also make your case more tangible.

Proposed Solution: Include the necessary information they need to understand your recommended product, service, or solution. Also include a full financial analysis, project and implementation plans, and team members. You'll also want to put in supporting documentation such as references, case studies, client list, charts of your revenue growth, analyst reports, and awards.

Appendix: This should include all those extra things that you think will be helpful, such as product brochures, marketing collateral, studies, articles about your company, legal documentation, or terminology.

If you go to all this work to create a good proposal, make sure you discuss it with your prospect first before you submit the final document. You can do this in person, on the phone, or via a Web conference.

This is an invaluable exercise. It ensures accuracy and alignment. You get additional insights you can use to strengthen your proposal. You uncover potential areas of contention between committee members and can thus make changes beforehand. You get a better sense of how your recommendations will be perceived. If you're working with multiple decision makers, invite several to give you some feedback prior to presenting the final proposal.

When frazzled prospects encounter a format that makes sense, you make it easier for them to go ahead with your proposal. Again, eliminating complexity always pays off. So does a strong business case that's aligned with their business needs. When you walk them through the proposal, you have an opportunity to bring your own personal value to the discussion, too.

Make It Easy to Say Yes

Finally, there are many strategies you can use that can make it easier for your prospects to give you the go-ahead. Savvy sellers think about them from the outset, not after they run into trouble with a decision getting stalled. In short, they're prepared.

You may want to consider some or all of these strategies to expedite getting the ink on paper:

Propose Fewer Options.

In fact, you might even think about proposing exactly what you recommend instead of three choices. The fewer decisions your prospect has to make, the easier it is. If you sense hesitation, ask what the concerns are. You can always come back with a second option that better meets their needs.

Break Your Offering Down into Small Pieces.

Sometimes prospects don't have any budget till the next month (quarter/year). Fiscal constraints prevent them from getting started. First, discover their current budget cycle. Then you might propose invoicing Phase 1 in Q3, Phase 2 in Q4, and Phase 3 in the following year. Prospects who want to work with you will find a way to make it happen.

Suggest More Bang-for-the-Buck.

Rather than lowering your pricing if your prospect balks, offer more value for the same financial investment. One thing I frequently propose to my price-sensitive clients is a pre-meeting or follow-up tele-seminar for their salespeople. This "sweetens the pot," making it easier for decision makers to say yes.

Adapt Ideas From Outside Your Industry.

At Media 1, a company that sells custom learning programs, CEO Chris Willis adapted a common retail BOGO ("buy one/get one") promotion for her corporate clients. Knowing that there were savings when they did multiple projects in close succession, she offered "economies of scale" pricing for add-on projects. Not only did this help her clients in tough times, but it also solidified her lifetime value with them.

Propose Creative Payment Solutions.

I've always been a big advocate of doing this—legally, of course. We sometimes get locked into our usual ways and forget that there are multiple options. When Rebecca Patt, VP of

Development for an executive search firm, was faced with a client who wanted to delay payment for months versus pay in thirty days, she was initially horrified. But after thinking about it, she came up with a strategy that allowed her client to delay payments partially, but yet maintain her cash flow. This led to additional contracts.

Put Some Skin in the Game.

Chris Peterson, president of BrandStand Marketing Group, suggests tying a portion of your compensation to the successful execution of the project and the achievement of mutually set, predefined results. But if you do this, he advises that you never assume more than half the risk. Otherwise, the project will fall short of expectations due to your client's lack of involvement.

Make Your Contracts Simpler.

Lawyer and business strategist Curt Sahakian frequently works with sales organizations to simplify their contracts in order to close deals. In addition to low word counts, he recommends putting the most important information up front, grouping all blanks together, and putting items requiring negotiation into exhibits.

Offer Payment Over Time.

Many small businesses don't have in-house leasing options for their customers. They make them go to the bank to get their own loans. That extra work just slows everything down. Contact and interview potential leasing agents who can meet with your prospects as soon as you give them the go-ahead.

You'll notice that none of these strategies discounts your price, at least in the traditional sense. Jumping on the price-cutting bandwagon before other options are explored sets a dangerous precedent. Yet each of these options keeps the conversation going, bringing you one step closer to agreement.

By keeping things simple, ensuring alignment with business objectives, and bringing your expertise to your prospect, you not only differentiate yourself from competitors but also keep your momentum going. Best of all, frazzled customers won't be able to resist you!

32

Success with the Third Decision

At long last, the decision is made! You've invested countless hours preparing and strategizing for each of the numerous meetings. You've given it your all, hoping you've done enough to come out on top.

Unfortunately, not everyone can be a winner. Should you lose, be gracious. Thank your prospects for the opportunity and wish them all the best. There's always the possibility that their selected resource won't work out. You want to be a viable option should that happen. Also, with today's social media, it's become a small world. You don't want to be written up as a sore loser on somebody's blog!

If you win, it's time to celebrate. I mean it. You deserve a pat on the back. It's even more rewarding when you've beaten out several formidable competitors. In the process, you convinced multiple decision makers that working with your company will yield the best possible outcomes with the least amount of risk.

And it's also time to get to work. Your new customers need

to know that you look forward to working with them. Your first official job is to tell them that you appreciate their business.

Making It Happen

Then it's time to dig in. Your customers decided to work with you for a reason. Now you need to live up to their expectations. Perhaps you need to get others in your organization involved now. Make sure it's a smooth transition. Do you have a delivery date to meet? Make sure things happen on time.

What about training and implementation? Any new system or methodology is bound to create strife when it's first introduced. People get frustrated; they want to go back to the old ways, which they were comfortable with. You need to manage the project realistically, making sure people know what to expect and when.

You are responsible for the success of this project, order, contract, or deal. Just because you won the business doesn't guarantee a long-term relationship with this customer. That needs to be earned. But it's also where the biggest payoff is.

Pay attention to detail, constantly monitor progress, and check on satisfaction levels. Make sure your project comes in on time and within budget. Should any changes arise that could alter expectations, deal with them openly and honestly. Your customers don't want any surprises.

Celebrate Your Customers' Successes

Ultimately, your success is dependent on your customers' success. Did they achieve their implementation milestones? Were their objectives met? How soon were they able to see their desired results? Did they get the cost savings they were hoping for? Were they able to reduce their operating expenses? How was revenue impacted?

This is why they chose you. They wanted you to make a difference for their company. In some cases, they'll be closely monitoring the results because they have the systems in place. But if they don't, you want to work with them on developing some metrics they can use to measure their success. Certainly, this is important for you, because this data becomes the substance of a future case study.

But it's really more important for your customers. They want to show their bosses and colleagues that they made a smart decision—one that paid off handsomely for the company. By helping them share their successes, you solidify your position in the account and develop loyal customers who love working with you.

Your first win in a company is, without a doubt, the hardest. When you make your customers' decision a resounding success, they expand their relationship with you. That makes all the hard work you put into winning their business worthwhile.

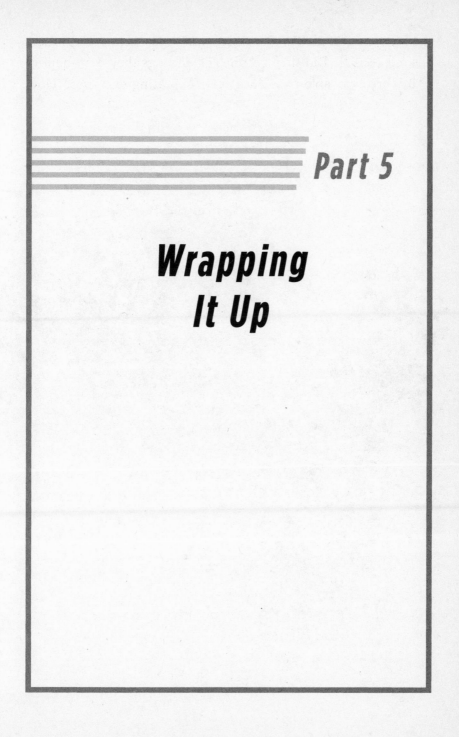

Part 5

Wrapping It Up

33

SNAP to It!

As I've shown you, selling in today's crazy-busy world is tough. Your prospects have fundamentally changed. You've learned that time is their most precious commodity and they protect it at all costs. If you won't pay the "price of admission" or if you fail to demonstrate personal value right up front, they'll refuse to meet with you. If they want to learn about your products or services, they'll check online. They have no use for self-serving salespeople who can't seem to ditch the pitch.

Not only that, these frazzled people will stay with the status quo for as long as they can—it's too disruptive to change. They don't need anything more on their to-do lists; they're too busy putting out fires and handling a much-too-big workload. Complexity of any sort sends them spiraling into overwhelm. It takes a strong business case to get them to change. And when they finally do take action, they worry about making risky, career-inhibiting decisions.

Unless you recognize how profound these changes are and you alter your behavior accordingly, you'll find yourself quickly and perennially consigned to the dreaded D-Zone.

What the Future Holds

In the upcoming years, it's not going to get any easier. The economy may improve, but unless something drastic happens, people will still be expected to do more with less. In a state of perpetual overwhelm, they'll be bombarded by overzealous marketers and sellers vying for their attention. The barriers to entry in an account will get even higher. And overwhelmed customers will continue to struggle with more work, fewer resources, and shorter deadlines.

But remember: Deep inside this corporate craziness lies the heart of opportunity.

Your prospects desperately want to work with smart, savvy people who bring them fresh ideas, insights, and information on how to achieve their business objectives. They crave working relationships with competent, caring, trustworthy individuals who can guide them through the decision-making process, minimizing any missteps. Keep in mind:

- When you align your offering with their critical business objectives, you capture and maintain your prospects' interest.
- When you bring personal value and expertise, you get chosen over competitors, fight fewer pricing battles, and increase customer loyalty.
- When you keep things simple, you make it easier for prospects to buy from you.

- When you raise priorities, your sales process goes much faster and you get the business with less competition.

Even in tough times, you can be successful when you master the skills, strategies, and mind-set of a SNAP seller.

Closing the SNAP Gap

At the foundation of your sales efforts is a solid understanding of your prospects' business, objectives, strategies, initiatives, and challenges. That's why the Buyer's Matrix is such a powerful tool. Get started on yours today.

But you'll have even greater success when you master the mind meld. Being able to think "as if" you were your prospects enables you to evaluate and improve your own sales approach prior to actually meeting with your customers. That's what the very best sellers do!

The great thing is you don't have to be a genius to do a mind meld. You just need to discipline yourself to take that one extra step before you act and ask, "What would Eric or Sarah or Alex think about this?"

Use the SNAP Check to evaluate their perceptions of your phone messages, meeting plans, presentations, proposals, and more. Have you made things simple enough or are they still too complex? Are you demonstrating your personal value or do you sound like every other seller? Have you aligned with their business objectives or is what you're offering irrelevant? Do you raise the priority status or is your offering still a nicety?

Be tough on yourself. It's how you avoid getting consigned to the dreaded D-Zone before you even get your foot in the door. It's also how you eliminate this response: "We decided to stay with the status quo" or "We've decided to go with your competitor."

Better yet, when you rigorously practice SNAP selling you'll hear: "Let's meet," "We've decided to change," and "You're the one we want to work with."

Success Is a Decision

When I first began my sales career, I didn't decide to become a superstar. That was unattainable. But I did see that it was possible to be at 100 percent of quota selling copiers for Xerox. So that's what I tackled first. Once I achieved that, I made a second decision: to become a top performer in our regional office. Then I decided to learn how to sell technology. After that, I decided to start my own sales training company.

Success was achieved one decision at a time. When you make that commitment, though, you're setting yourself up for challenging times. You'll make dozens of mistakes. You'll sound like a babbling fool. Sometimes you'll embarrass yourself beyond belief. And you'll doubt that success is even possible.

I'll never forget when I cold-called Tinsey, the administrative assistant. Her company needed a new copier, and she told me she was the one making the decision. Shortly after our first meeting, I read a book on selling to top-level decision makers and concluded that I should talk to her boss instead. So I set up an appointment directly with him. Of course, Tinsey was there to greet me when I arrived. She was furious that I'd gone behind her back and laid into me with a four-letter-word-filled tirade like I'd never heard before.

I was mortified, knowing I'd made an error from which

it was impossible to recover. I fainted. Dead away on the tiled floor. I came to with the office staff hovering over me. After Tinsey found out that I was okay, she suggested I leave and never come back. I never did.

That was only one of the days when I wanted to quit selling. Instead, I made a decision. I'd chosen to succeed in sales—to figure out how to make it in this crazy career. So I literally picked myself up off the floor, brushed myself off, and challenged myself to learn from that embarrassing situation.

You see, there is no failure in life—only many valuable learning experiences. Each time you encounter one, you have three options:

1. Quit because it's too darn hard or painful, which means you'll never achieve your goals.

2. Keep doing the same thing, thus ensuring that you'll experience the same problems again.

3. Figure out what works, even if you have to experiment for a while to find the answer.

You can't "try" to be successful at selling. It just doesn't work. You have to commit to it and be willing to do what it takes to reach your objectives. Then, when things change, you have to go back to learning again.

Perhaps that's why I've always been inspired by Edgar Guest's poem "It Couldn't Be Done," which starts out like this:

> *Somebody said that it couldn't be done,*
> *But he with a chuckle replied*
> *That "maybe it couldn't" but he would be the one*

Who wouldn't say so till he'd tried.
So he buckled right in with the trace of a grin
on his face. If he worried he hid it.
He started to sing as he tackled the thing
That couldn't be done and he did it.

We all love that thrill of accomplishment. Just think how long it's been since you had that exuberant "Yes!" feeling that comes when you nail something for the first time. You know how much you deserve it!

Of course, you don't have to change. That just means you'll have to work harder and harder each year just to stay even. Ultimately, you'll probably get burned out or kicked out.

Like Pollyanna, I prefer to look at the good side of things. You'll have lots of opportunity to stretch yourself, test your skills, become more creative, collaborate, and more. My intent in writing *SNAP Selling* is to show you what it takes to be successful in the upcoming years.

However, the decision to grow beyond your comfort zone is all yours. It's one that requires a greater commitment than most sellers are willing to make.

But it's all worth it when you get to the other side. Prospects will want to meet with you. They'll willingly open up about their business objectives, needs, and issues. They'll rely on your guidance in making their decisions—and will make them faster. They'll choose to work with you, even if it costs them more. Finally, because they trust your judgment, you'll get even more business from them and others whom they refer to you.

Yes, success is a choice. When you make that decision to live by the SNAP Rules, every ounce of your effort will be paid back many times over. It's worth it!

ACKNOWLEDGMENTS

I'VE BEEN GREATLY BLESSED by the many people in my life who've inspired me to do things I initially thought were impossible and who supported me in turning them into a reality.

You're one of them! I'm humbled that you look to me for advice on how to be more successful. It's because of you that I write. Without you, *SNAP Selling* would still be a figment of my imagination. Thank you for sharing your stories with me, for asking me questions, and for letting me know that I make a difference.

Many thanks to my clients, too. I appreciate the opportunity to help your sales teams discover what it takes to be successful in today's business environment. Your trust in me keeps me at the top of my game, and your salespeople keep me fresh.

I'd also like to honor the sales luminaries who came before me. As Sir Isaac Newton once said, "If I have seen further, it is by standing on the shoulders of giants." I am grateful for the work of Neil Rackham, Larry Wilson, Linda Richardson, Tony Parinello, Dale Carnegie, Barbara Geraghty, Mike Bosworth, Sharon Drew Morgen, and Og Mandino.

I am indebted to my family for surrounding me with love and support. Thanks to my husband, Fred, who gave me the confidence to start my own business years ago—and who still can't quite believe the whirlwind he set in motion. He's my grounding rod who keeps me focused on what's most important in life. My children, Katie and Ryan, make sure I stay open to change, teach me new lessons every day, and keep me young! My mother, Pat Ulseth, taught me (an introvert) how to be social, the importance of good grammar, and how to write like Dr. Seuss. And my father, Jack Ulseth, a brilliant engineer, showed me that it's okay to step off the corporate career path to follow your passion.

Many thanks to all the awesome women in my life. Talent expert Faith Ralston and eMarketing strategist Ardath Albee are my creative muses, closest advisers, and best friends. They keep me on track and on purpose. I'm also grateful for the support of these incredibly talented sales experts: Kendra Lee, Anne Miller, Kim Duke, Colleen Francis, Lori Richardson, Leslie Buterin, Colleen Stanley, Brooke Green, Jill Harrington, Nancy Bleeke, Lynn Hidy, Joanne Black, Wendy Weiss, Debbie Mrazek, Josiane Feigon, Danita Bye, Molly Cox, and Nancy Nardin. We've brainstormed together, grown together, and cheered for one another. A special thanks to my friends Mary Kath, Marci Heerman, Rita Webster, Susan Zimmerman, and Judy Lovold for always being there for me.

I want to acknowledge all the wonderful guys in my life, too. In the sales field, I have tons of respect for these talented colleagues and friends who have stimulated my thinking, supported my work, and given me great feedback: Dave Stein, Charlie Green, Keith Rosen, Jeb Blount, Tom Sant, Mike McLaughlin, Jonathan Farrington, Mark Hunter, Nigel Edelshain, Lee Salz, Sam Richter, Mike Schultz, Jonathan London, Michael Nick, Josh Gordon, Nick Miller, Bill Caskey, Kelley Robertson, Paul McCord, Waldo Waldman, David Brock, Dan Seidman, and Brian Carroll.

Other business colleagues who have been immensely helpful to me in the past few years include: Robin Fray Carey, Genevieve Bos, John Jantsch, Larry Benet, Michael Stelzner, Eric Gagnon, Michael Port,

David Meerman Scott, Bob Burg, and Robert Middleton. Many thanks also to Dwayne Walker, who reserved the Web address snapselling .com years ago, but saved it for me!

This book itself wouldn't be possible without my agent, Ethan Freidman, from LevelFiveMedia. He helped me write a rock-solid proposal and land a contract with a top-notch publisher. I couldn't be happier. And I so appreciate my wonderful editor, Brooke Carey, whose eagle eye spotted every shortcoming in my manuscript. Under her expert guidance, we created a book I'm proud to have written.

Finally, I want to thank Steve Peterson, my childhood friend who passed away fifteen years ago. In our last conversation, which occurred while he was in hospice, he helped me realize the importance of sharing what I know with the world.

APPENDIX

SALES 2.0 RESOURCES

To be successful in selling today, you need to be using Sales 2.0 tools.*
In short, these productivity-enhancing technologies and processes help
you speed up your sales cycle, find quality leads, drive more profitable
deals, and reduce competition.

They do this by:

* Enabling you to pinpoint the right prospects and the right
  time;
* Slashing the time it takes you to find relevant, timely information that ensures you're focused on high-priority issues
  and aligned with key corporate initiatives; and
* Tracking prospect interest and activity, enabling you to follow up with appropriate messaging when someone is most
  interested.

---

* Sales 2.0 is a registered trademark of Sales 2.0 LLC.

Throughout this book, I've mentioned numerous Sales 2.0 resources. In this section, I bring them all together and add a few more. While many of these companies started as stand-alone firms, technology is now enabling them to integrate applications within applications. The result? Incredibly powerful sales productivity and effectiveness tools.

DISCLAIMER: These Sales 2.0 resources do *not* take the place of good selling skills. Instead, they enhance and complement them. You need both to excel.

LEAD DATABASES, DECISION MAKER'S NAMES

Use these services to identify the right people to contact within your target market, and to learn their e-mail address, phone numbers, and other information. By setting specific parameters, you can compile a highly focused list to use for prospecting:

Jigsaw	ZoomInfo
Dow Jones	Hoovers
OneLead	OneSource
NetProspex	ZapData
Datasentials	Demandbase

You can also get detailed information about individuals and targeted accounts with ZoomInfo, D&B Hoovers, and Dow Jones. Many public libraries have subscriptions to these sites, so you can access them for free.

TRIGGER ALERTS AND CONNECTIONS

With these subscription-based services, you receive alerts whenever your predefined trigger events occur. You can get a jump on your competition, prioritize hot opportunities, and find invaluable connections. Also, everything can be fully integrated into your CRM system.

- InsideView: Take a look at SalesView Pro or Team; multiple levels of services are available;

- Dow Jones: Check out Companies and Executives Sales; primarily for medium-to-large firms; and
- SalesFuel: Primarily for small- to medium-size firms.

ALERT SERVICES
With these free services, you set trigger event parameters (including news updates from targeted companies) and are notified when they occur. Sometimes the sheer number of alerts can get overwhelming.

- RSS feeds of company Web sites
- Business Journals: bizjournals.com
- Google Alerts: google.com/alerts
- Yahoo Alerts: alerts.yahoo.com

SPECIALTY SALES INTELLIGENCE
Check out these options for deeper or more specialized information that you can find through traditional sources. Also, you can get information from a variety of sources compiled into one report.

- First Research: Reports on various industries, market analysis, trend predictions, pre-call prep guidelines, and more;
- SalesQuest: Deep sales intelligence for enterprise software and IT services companies; and
- Industry Gems: Strategic account intelligence for selling to large corporations.

SOCIAL NETWORKING

You can use these online interest-sharing communities to connect with prospects or customers, initiate conversations, learn, share perspectives, and much more. The content on these sites is user-created:

LinkedIn	Facebook
Blogs: company and personal	Twitter
BizNik	PerfectNetworker
GreenlightCommunity	Ning

SALES ENABLEMENT

These Sales 2.0 tools help you be more productive, find information faster, and make connections easier.

- ConnectandSell: Get your reps on the phone talking to hot prospects, not voice-mail messages.
- Xobni: Organize your Outlook contacts, follow e-mail threads, and identify more connections.
- YouSendIt: Use this quick, easy, and secure service to send big files or folders.
- SlideRocket: Make and manage knock-your-socks-off presentations with this new technology.
- Brainshark: Create voice-enriched presentations to promote your expertise or business.
- SantCorp: Use these customized databases to quickly build customized RFPs or proposals.

E-MAIL TECHNOLOGIES

It's imperative today to maintain regular contact with customers and prospects. That's why so many companies and salespeople use these e-mail programs to share their expertise, build stronger connections, and ensure visibility at just the right time:

Exact Target

aWeber

iContact

Constant Contact

MailChimp

To send individual e-mails that include both voice and visuals such as video, PowerPoint, or graphics, check out ConnectNote, Proclaim (from NetBriefings), and GoldMail. To know when your prospects read your e-mails, reopen, or forward them, check out ReadNotify.

E-MEETINGS

Because your prospects are so busy, many now prefer to have online meetings with you prior to setting up a longer appointment. Using these tools also makes you much more productive.

GoToMeeting	GoToWebinar
Webex	BrainShark

INTERNET LEAD GENERATION

These Sales 2.0 technologies enable you to identify companies who are already looking on your Web site and what they're interested in. The key to success is to have an information-rich Web site that people find valuable, stick around to read, and come back to visit again.

With these tools, you get an alert whenever a "meaningful event" occurs, such as a prospect downloading a white paper or visiting your site for the third time in one week. When you know people are interested, you can engage with them when they're hot.

LeadLander	Netfactor
LeadsExplorer	LeadForce1
ActiveProspects	

MARKETING AUTOMATION

In today's business environment, savvy companies are using eMarketing strategies to craft personalized communications to prospects based on their behavior, interests, and characteristics. Marketing nurtures the prospects until they're considered sales-ready, then turns them over to Sales. When you get these leads, you'll also get invaluable data, such as what your prospects clicked on, read, reread, or forwarded—and how much time they invested doing this.

HubSpot	Genius
Marketo	Genoo

Eloqua	PinPointe
ActiveConversion	Manticore Technology

Using these tools, combined with quality content results in higher-quality prospects who are knowledgeable about your offering, interested in your company, and seriously considering taking action.

A DAY IN THE LIFE OF A SALES 2.0 SELLER

Mike Damphousse of Green Leads is the consummate sales and marketing person. He's an industry leader in the demand generation market and sells primarily to high-tech companies. His firm uses a variety of Sales 2.0 technologies to generate leads, nurture relationships, identify opportunities, research prospects, and much more.

Here's an everyday example of how he uses Sales 2.0 tools to maximize his sales effectiveness:

> When I get to the office in the morning, I turn on my Sales 2.0 cockpit and get to work. I work with two monitors. The right one has these applications open at all times: LinkedIn, Jigsaw, LeadLander and HubSpot. The left one is where I work e-mails, Salesforce.com (my CRM system) and documents.
>
> After going through my e-mail in the morning, I focus on leads. First, I check LeadLander to find out the companies (not individuals) that have visited our site in the past day. I can tell what they looked at and for how long. For example, if someone from a midsized firm read three blog articles, looked at our Appointment Setting page and then our Contact page—that's potentially a huge opportunity for us.
>
> At that point, I go into LinkedIn and Jigsaw to identify decision makers in Marketing—which is where we go to get our foot in the door. If the company isn't too large, I can typically identify two to four names. I add them to my prospect list and then start initiating contact via phone and e-mail.
>
> Then I look at HubSpot, which is an inbound lead engine. When a prospect fills out a form on our Web site to get any

kind of information, I can see every page they look at. So let's say that someone subscribed to our blog three months ago and have been getting updates every time we publish an article. But then one morning, I see that they visited a handful of pages on the site including our Self Serve Meetings page. That indicates they might be thinking about purchasing some introductory appointments. Suddenly, they're a hot prospect—first on my list for that day. If I sent them an e-mail, I can tell if it caught their attention, too, because I get a report on that.

Later in the day, after I've been making my outbound sales calls, I get a Google Alert that one of my existing clients just issued a press release indicating a new product initiative with the Healthcare market. I know they've never gone after this business before, but my contact in marketing hasn't brought this campaign to my attention yet. So, I fire off an e-mail mentioning the press release and suggest how we can help them jumpstart the program. She's responsive, and within 15 seconds my phone rings. Now I'm expanding my services within an existing account.

This is just a snapshot of what my day is like. I'm constantly researching prospects, gathering sales intelligence on their business, then making calls or following up. Plus, by focusing on companies already interested in our services or who have relevant trigger events, I really maximize my time.

By using these Sales 2.0 tools combined with strong selling skills, Mike's business is thriving even during tough economic times. What doesn't show up in his story is how effectively he uses his deep knowledge of his prospect's business, background, and online behaviors to align with their interests, simplify his messaging, and demonstrate the personal value he brings to client relationships. In short, he follows the SNAP Rules.

RECOMMENDED READING

I'm frequently asked which books I recommend for sellers. Here are some of my favorites. All offer strong how-to advice to increase your sales.

B2B SALES CLASSICS

The Greatest Salesman in the World, Og Mandino, Bantam Books, 1974
Major Account Sales Strategies, Neil Rackham, McGraw-Hill, 1989
The New Strategic Selling, Robert Miller, Stephen Heiman, and Tad Tuleja, Business Plus (updated), 2005
Selling to VITO, the Very Important Top Officer, Anthony Parinello, Adams Media, 1999
Selling with Integrity, Sharon Drew Morgen, Berkley Books, 1999
Solution Selling, Michael Bosworth, McGraw-Hill, 1994
SPIN Selling, Neil Rackham, McGraw-Hill, 1988

B2B SALES SUCCESS

42 Rules for Growing Enterprise Revenue, Lilia Shirman, SuperStar Press, 2009
42 Rules of Cold Calling Executives, Mari Anne Vanella, SuperStar Press, 2008
Accelerants, Michael Boylan, Portfolio, 2007
Closing Time, Rob Hubsher, Sales Optimization Group, 2009
Dirty Little Secrets, Sharon Drew Morgen, 2009
The Entrepreneur's Guide to Selling, Jonathan London, Praeger, 2009
Exceptional Selling, Jeff Thull, Wiley, 2006
The Field Guide to Sales, Debbie Mrazek, Bee Press, 2008
Heavy Hitter Selling, Steve Martin, Wiley, 2006
Honesty Sells, Steven Gaffney and Colleen Francis, Wiley, 2009
How to Sell When Nobody's Buying, Dave Lakhani, Wiley, 2009
Little Red Book of Selling, Jeffrey Gitomer, Bard Press, 2004
Let's Get Real or Let's Not Play, Mahan Khalsa and Randy Illig, Portfolio, 2008

Metaphorically Selling, Anne Miller, Chiron, 2003
Negotiation Rules!, Jeanette Nyden, Sales Gravy Press, 2009
Perfect Selling, Linda Richardson, McGraw-Hill, 2008
Questions That Sell, Paul Cherry, AMACOM, 2006
The Secrets of Power Selling, Kelley Robertson, Wiley 2007
Secrets of Question-Based Selling, Thomas Freese, Sourcebooks, 2000
Sell Smarter, Justyn Howard, TPP, 2009
Selling Against the Goal, Kendra Lee, Kaplan, 2005.
Selling 2.0, Josh Gordon, Berkley Trade, 2000
Selling to Big Companies, Jill Konrath, Kaplan, 2006
Selling to the C-Suite, Nicholas A. C. Read and Stephen J. Bistritz, McGraw-Hill, 2009
Smart Selling on the Phone and Online, Josiane Feigon, AMACOM, 2009
Take the Cold Out of Cold Calling, Sam Richter, Beaver Pond Press, 2009

NETWORKING | REFERRALS

Endless Referrals, Bob Burg, McGraw-Hill, 2006
How to Really Use LinkedIn, Jan Vermeiren, BookSurge, 2009
I'm on LinkedIn, Now What???, Jason Alba, 2009
Me 2.0, Dan Schawbel, Kaplan, 2009
Never Eat Alone, Keith Ferrazzi, Broadway Business, 2005
No More Cold Calling, Joanne Black, Business Plus, 2007
The Referral Engine, John Jantsch, Portfolio, 2010

PROPOSALS

The Language of Success, Tom Sant, AMACOM, 2008
Persuasive Business Proposals, Tom Sant, AMACOM, 2003
RFPs Suck!, Tom Searcy, Channel V Books, 2009

PRESENTATIONS

The Back of the Napkin, Dan Roam, Portfolio, 2008
Beyond Bullet Points, Cliff Atkinson, Microsoft Press, 2007

Great Demo!, Peter Cohan, iUniverse, 2005
Persuasive Presentations, Nick Souter, Sterling, 2007
Presentation Zen, Garr Reynolds, New Riders Press, 2008
Presentation Zen Design, Garr Reynolds, New Riders Press, 2009
Slide:ology, Nancy Duarte, O'Reilly Media, 2008
The Virtual Presenter's Handbook, Roger Courville, 1080 Group, 2009

SELLING PROFESSIONAL SERVICES

Beyond Booked Solid, Michael Port, Wiley, 2008
Book Yourself Solid, Michael Port, Wiley, 2008
Get Clients Now!, C. J. Hayden, AMACOM, 2007
Guerrilla Marketing for Consultants, Jay Conrad Levinson and Mike W. McLaughlin, Wiley, 2004
How to Become a Rainmaker, Jeffrey J. Fox, Hyperion, 2000
Trust-Based Selling, Charles H. Green, McGraw-Hill, 2005
Winning the Professional Services Sale, Michael W. McLaughlin, Wiley, 2009

B2B MARKETING BOOKS

Duct Tape Marketing, John Jantsch, Thomas Nelson, 2008
eMarketing Strategies for the Complex Sale, Ardath Albee, McGraw-Hill, 2009
Lead Generation for the Complex Sale, Brian Carroll, McGraw-Hill, 2006
New Rules of Marketing and PR, David Meerman Scott, Wiley, 2007
Professional Services Marketing, Mike Schultz and John Doerr, Wiley, 2009
World Wide Rave, David Meerman Scott, Wiley, 2009
Writing White Papers, Michael Stelzner, WhitePaperSource, 2006

SALES MOTIVATION

The Go-Giver, Bob Burg and John David Mann, Portfolio, 2007
Never Fly Solo, Robert "Waldo" Waldman, McGraw-Hill, 2009
PowerPrinciples, Jeb Blount, Palm Tree Press, 2007
Sales Autopsy, Dan Seidman, Kaplan, 2006

SALES MANAGEMENT

Coaching Salespeople into Sales Champions, Keith Rosen, Wiley, 2008
Growing Great Sales Teams, Colleen Stanley, Heartland Press, 2006
Managing Major Sales, Neil Rackham, Harper Business, 1991
Sales Coaching, Linda Richardson, McGraw-Hill, 2008
Soar Despite Your Dodo Sales Manager, Lee B. Salz, Wbusiness Books, 2007
The Ultimate Sales Machine, Chet Holmes, Portfolio, 2008

RELATED BOOKS

Brain Rules, John J. Medina, Pear Press, 2008
buy•ology, Martin Lindstrom, Doubleday, 2008
CrazyBusy, Edward M. Hollowell, M.D., Ballantine , 2007
Hare Brain, Tortoise Mind, Guy Claxton, Ecco Press, 1999
In Praise of Slowness, Carl Honore, HarperCollins, 2004
Made to Stick, Chip and Dan Heath, Random House, 2007
The Paradox of Choice: Why More Is Less, Barry Schwartz, HarperPerennial, 2004
A Sense of Urgency, John P. Kotter, Harvard Business Press, 2008
Simplicity: The New Competitive Advantage, Bill Jensen, Perseus Books, 2000
SWAY: The Irresistible Pull of Irrational Behavior, Ori and and Rom Brafman, Doubleday, 2008
A Whole New Mind, Daniel Pink, Riverhead Trade, 2006

SALES WEB SITES

To learn more about sales training companies, sales experts, and authors, visit their Web sites and blogs.

AllBusiness.com	SalesPond.com
EyesOnSales.com	SalesPractice.com
JustSell.com	SellingPower.com
SalesDog.com	SellingtoBigCompanies.com
SalesGravy.com	TheCustomerCollective.com
Salesopedia.com	

Many top sales experts, trainers, and authors have their own blogs that you might want to check out, too.

GOBBLEDYGOOK GRADER

This free online tool from HubSpot helps you permanently eliminate jargon, clichés, and overused, hype-filled words from your sales vocabulary. It works well for press releases, sales letters, e-mails, and online copy. Get your Gobbledygook grade together with a full report on what you can do to improve your message: gobbledygook.grader.com.

INDEX